TENTING TONIGHT

The Soldier's Life

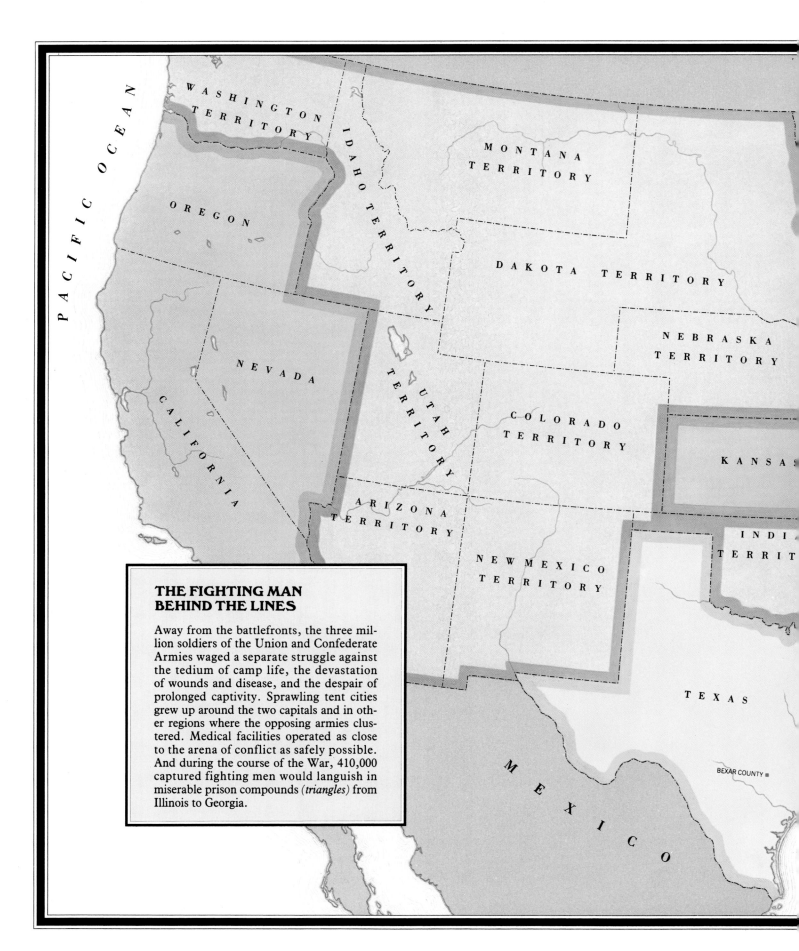

THE FIGHTING MAN BEHIND THE LINES

Away from the battlefronts, the three million soldiers of the Union and Confederate Armies waged a separate struggle against the tedium of camp life, the devastation of wounds and disease, and the despair of prolonged captivity. Sprawling tent cities grew up around the two capitals and in other regions where the opposing armies clustered. Medical facilities operated as close to the arena of conflict as safely possible. And during the course of the War, 410,000 captured fighting men would languish in miserable prison compounds (*triangles*) from Illinois to Georgia.

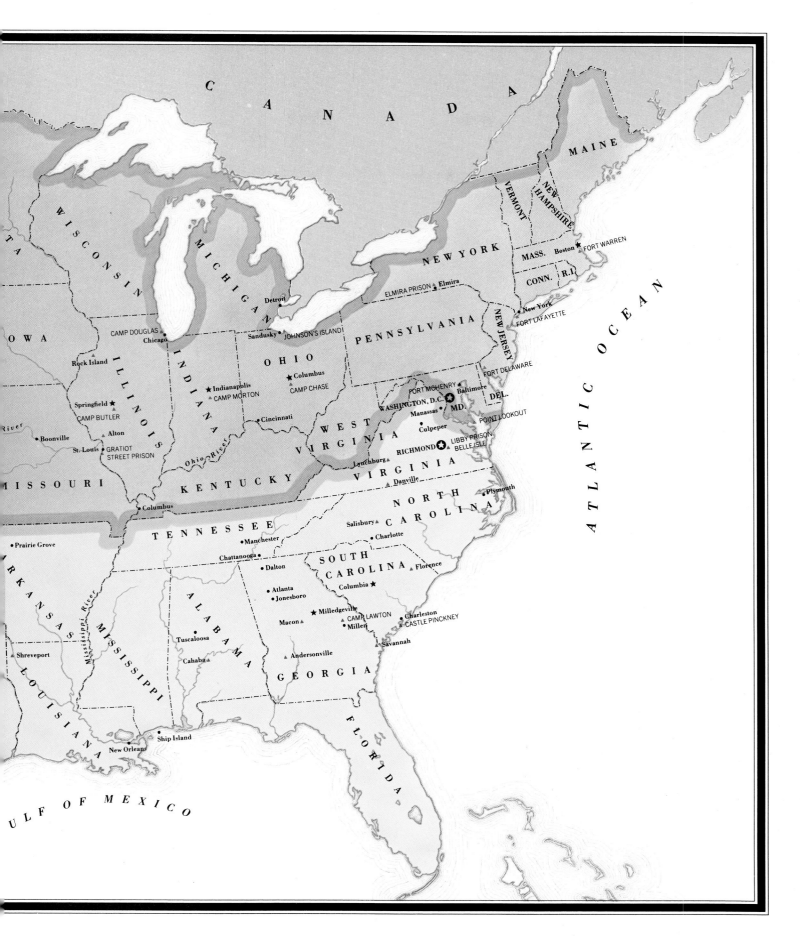

Other Publications:

THE ENCHANTED WORLD
THE KODAK LIBRARY OF CREATIVE PHOTOGRAPHY
GREAT MEALS IN MINUTES
PLANET EARTH
COLLECTOR'S LIBRARY OF THE CIVIL WAR
LIBRARY OF HEALTH
CLASSICS OF THE OLD WEST
THE EPIC OF FLIGHT
THE GOOD COOK
THE SEAFARERS
WORLD WAR II
HOME REPAIR AND IMPROVEMENT
THE OLD WEST
LIFE LIBRARY OF PHOTOGRAPHY (revised)
LIFE SCIENCE LIBRARY (revised)

For information on and a full description of any of the
Time-Life Books series listed above, please write:
Reader Information, Time-Life Books
541 North Fairbanks Court, Chicago, Illinois 60611

This volume is one of a series that chronicles in full the
events of the American Civil War, 1861-1865.
Other books in the series include:
Brother against Brother: The War Begins
First Blood: Fort Sumter to Bull Run
The Blockade: Runners and Raiders
The Road to Shiloh: Early Battles in the West
Forward to Richmond: McClellan's Peninsular Campaign
Decoying the Yanks: Jackson's Valley Campaign
Confederate Ordeal: The Southern Home Front
Lee Takes Command: From Seven Days to Second Bull Run
The Coastal War: Chesapeake Bay to Rio Grande

The Cover: On a cold, drizzly day early in the War,
Federal soldiers bivouacked near Washington, D.C.,
boil coffee and cook their rations over a campfire,
while officers in a rain-drenched tent share a meal.

THE CIVIL WAR

TENTING TONIGHT

BY

JAMES I. ROBERTSON JR.

AND THE

EDITORS OF TIME-LIFE BOOKS

The Soldier's Life

TIME-LIFE BOOKS, ALEXANDRIA, VIRGINIA

Time-Life Books Inc.
is a wholly owned subsidiary of

TIME INCORPORATED

FOUNDER: Henry R. Luce 1898-1967

Editor-in-Chief: Henry Anatole Grunwald
President: J. Richard Munro
Chairman of the Board: Ralph P. Davidson
Corporate Editor: Jason McManus
Group Vice President, Books: Joan D. Manley

TIME-LIFE BOOKS INC.

EDITOR: George Constable
Executive Editor: George Daniels
Director of Design: Louis Klein
Editorial Board: Roberta R. Conlan, Ellen Phillips,
Gerry Schremp, Gerald Simons, Rosalind Stubenberg,
Kit van Tulleken, Henry Woodhead
Director of Research: Phyllis K. Wise
Director of Photography: John Conrad Weiser

PRESIDENT: Reginald K. Brack Jr.
Senior Vice President: William Henry
Vice Presidents: George Artandi, Stephen L. Bair,
Robert A. Ellis, Juanita T. James, Christopher T. Linen,
James L. Mercer, Joanne A. Pello, Paul R. Stewart

The Civil War

Series Director: Henry Woodhead
Designer: Herbert H. Quarmby
Chief Researcher: Philip Brandt George

Editorial Staff for *Tenting Tonight*
Associate Editors: Thomas A. Lewis, R. W. Murphy
(text); Jane N. Coughran (pictures)
Staff Writers: Jan Leslie Cook, Allan Fallow,
David Johnson, Glenn McNatt, John Newton
Researchers: Harris J. Andrews, Susan V. Kelly
(principals); Stephanie A. Lewis, Gwen C. Mullen,
Brian C. Pohanka
Assistant Designer: Cynthia T. Richardson
Copy Coordinators: Elizabeth Graham,
Stephen G. Hyslop
Editorial Assistants: Audrey Prior Keir,
Andrea E. Reynolds
Special Contributor: Paula York-Soderlund

Editorial Operations
Design: Ellen Robling (assistant director)
Copy Room: Diane Ullius
Production: Anne B. Landry (director), Celia Beattie
Quality Control: James J. Cox (director), Sally Collins
Library: Louise D. Forstall

Correspondents: Elisabeth Kraemer-Singh (Bonn);
Margot Hapgood, Dorothy Bacon (London); Miriam
Hsia (New York); Maria Vincenza Aloisi, Josephine
du Brusle (Paris); Ann Natanson (Rome). Valuable
assistance was also provided by: Juliette Tomlinson
(Boston); Carolyn Chubet (New York).

The Author:
James I. Robertson Jr. is C. P. Miles Professor of History
at Virginia Tech. The recipient of the Nevins-Freeman
Award and other prizes in the field of Civil War history, he
has written or edited some 20 books, which include *The
Stonewall Brigade, Civil War Books: A Critical Bibliography*
and *Civil War Sites in Virginia*.

The Consultants:
Colonel John R. Elting, USA (Ret.), a former Associate
Professor at West Point, is the author of *Battles for Scandinavia* in the Time-Life Books World War II series and of
The Battle of Bunker's Hill, The Battles of Saratoga, Military History and Atlas of the Napoleonic Wars and *American
Army Life*. He is also editor of the three volumes of *Military Uniforms in America, 1755-1867*, and associate editor
of *The West Point Atlas of American Wars*.

William A. Frassanito, a Civil War historian and lecturer
specializing in photograph analysis, is the author of two
award-winning studies, *Gettysburg: A Journey in Time* and
*Antietam: The Photographic Legacy of America's Bloodiest
Day*, and a companion volume, *Grant and Lee, The Virginia Campaigns*. He has also served as chief consultant to the
photographic history series *The Image of War*.

Les Jensen, Curator of the U.S. Army Transportation
Museum at Fort Eustis, Virginia, specializes in Civil War
artifacts and is a conservator of historic flags. He is a
contributor to *The Image of War* series, consultant for
numerous Civil War publications and museums, and a
member of the Company of Military Historians. He was
formerly Curator of the Museum of the Confederacy in
Richmond, Virginia.

Michael McAfee specializes in military uniforms and has
been Curator of Uniforms and History at the West Point
Museum since 1970. A fellow of the Company of Military
Historians, he coedited with Colonel Elting *Long Endure:
The Civil War Years*, and he collaborated with Frederick
Todd on *American Military Equipage*. He is the author of
Artillery of the American Revolution, 1775-1783, and has
written numerous articles for *Military Images Magazine*.

Library of Congress Cataloguing in Publication Data
Robertson, James I.
    Tenting tonight.
    (The Civil War)
    Bibliography: p.
    Includes index.
    1. United States. Army — History — Civil War,
1861-1865. 2. Confederate States of America. Army —
History. 3. United States. Army — Military life.
4. United States — History — Civil War., 1861-1865.
I. Time-Life Books.   II. Title.   III. Series.
E491.R58 1984   973.7'84   84-8465
ISBN 0-8094-4736-3
ISBN 0-8094-4737-1 (lib. bdg.)

CONTENTS

Biding Time between Battles

"I am now very comfortably situated for the winter," a Confederate private wrote his mother in 1863, "having a very nice chimney attached to my tent, and everything that tends to make this unhappy life pleasant and agreeable." Not all were so fortunate, but millions of fighting men North and South made the best of life in camp, finding what comfort they could amid the hardship and tedium of soldiering.

In summer the troops slept in canvas tents, often so cramped that when one man rolled over, the rest had to follow suit. Some Confederates lacked shelter of any kind; they rigged open-air beds by heaping straw or leaves between two logs. In autumn, when the men took up winter quarters, those who could find wood built crude huts, laying split logs on the earth floor and fashioning bunks with mattresses of pine needles. In the absence of canvas or logs, men sought protection from the cold by excavating what they called "gopher holes" in the sides of hills or ravines.

When not drilling or standing guard, the troops read, played cards and wrote letters. In winter they might stage spirited snowball fights, the opposing units arrayed in battle formation with colors flying. Soldiers even made sporting use of a common pest, picking lice and racing them on patches of tent canvas or the flat sides of canteens.

Yet the War was never far away, and the men who had tasted battle grew to cherish their peaceful interludes in camp. Snug in winter quarters near Morristown, Tennessee, in 1863, a Confederate soldier damned his marching orders as "the demon of all our ease and happiness."

As his messmates look on, a Federal soldier takes time out from chopping firewood beside a mud-daubed winter hut near Falls Church, Virginia, in February 1863. The company cook — or "dogrobber," as he was often called — stands beside a former slave, hired as cookhouse servant.

Company A of the 5th Georgia Volunteers and their black camp servant lounge before a wall tent in this damaged photograph, taken at Augusta, Georgia, in 1861. The letters *CR* on the front of the tent stand for Clinch Rifles, the company's informal name.

Seated in the shade in church pews, Federal troops pass the time in camp writing letters, while a fellow soldier mends his clothes. Soldiers carried sewing kits called housewives and took pride in their skill; one boasted of patching his trousers "as good as a heap of women would do."

Men of the 1st Texas Brigade engage in a variety of chores — scrubbing clothes, frying corn pone and chopping firewood — outside their winter quarters at Camp Quantico, Virginia, in 1861. The log hut was opulent by Army standards, featuring a roof of sturdy shingles and a glass window with nearly every pane intact.

Four officers of the 114th Pennsylvania Infantry enjoy a quiet smoke, a hand of cards and bottles of wine brought by servants in their camp near Petersburg, Virginia, in August 1864. Some men were known to play cards just about every free moment.

14

Beneath an arbor, a Federal soldier receives a haircut from an amateur barber. After long campaigns, the men looked forward to such amenities; one Confederate recalled that "the luxury of a shave completed the restoration of the man to decency."

In this rare photograph, Federals attend a Negro minstrel show, one of the most popular forms of entertainment among troops in camp. The band consists, from right to left, of a tambourine player, a banjo player, two guitarists and a minstrel rattling a pair of rib bones in each hand.

Confederate artillerymen play cards beside a tree at their picket post on the Stono River near Charleston in 1861. At left, four slaves prepare a meal in a kettle.

Officers of the 164th New York fish and loll along Pope's Run near Sangster's Station, Virginia, as three Federal sentries guard the railroad bridge above.

17

Led by a drummer and their company commander, soldiers of the 22nd New York State Militia drill in a column of fours near Harpers Ferry, Virginia, in

.862. Drill was universally unpopular with the troops. "Between drills," quipped a soldier from Pennsylvania, "we drill, and sometimes stop to eat a little."

Answering the Call

When the Civil War erupted and the call for volunteers was sounded across the land, the respondents on both sides harbored a "fancy idea," as Confederate artilleryman Carlton McCarthy put it, "that the principal occupation of a soldier should be actual conflict with the enemy." They had been charged by emotional oratory to expect a rush to battle, a few days of hard fighting and a triumphant return home. Instead, the War dragged on for years, and for every day they spent in battle, the soldiers of North and South alike passed weeks, even months, fighting such prosaic enemies as heat, cold, mud, dust, loneliness and, worst of all at times, tedium. "War," observed Captain Oliver Wendell Holmes Jr. of the 20th Massachusetts Infantry, "is an organized bore."

The recruits of 1861 who answered the romantic call of flag and country were no better prepared for these everyday realities of war than they were for the shock of combat. Few of them had ever before gathered by the thousands in camps, slept under canvas or the stars for months at a time, marched in step, followed obscure orders or lived constrained by rigid discipline. The mysteries of army food were still unrevealed to them. So were the harsh realities of the medical treatment awaiting the sick and wounded, and the grim prisons that would hold the captured.

During the four years of war, Federal and Confederate fighting men would set an example of sacrifice that would rarely be surpassed. They did not seek to become professional soldiers. Most thought of themselves simply as civilians temporarily in service to their country. Their deeply ingrained traits of independence, humor and fear of God could not be quenched, even by the stultifying routine of army life.

Paradoxically, the men found in the most mundane of their hardships some of their most treasured memories. "Let us together recall with pleasure the past!" exclaimed artilleryman McCarthy years later. "Once more be hungry, and eat; once more tired, and rest; once more thirsty, and drink; once more cold and wet, let us sit by the roaring fire and let comfort creep over us." They recorded their triumphs over various adversities in letters, diaries, histories — even sketches and paintings — creating an unprecedented record of the common soldier's life between battles. Thus the troops themselves ensured remembrance of what McCarthy feared would be obscured by the boastful memoirs of leaders and the florid battle narratives of journalists: "How the hungry private fried his bacon, baked his biscuit, smoked his pipe."

At the beginning of the War, the main concern of most recruits was to reach the battlefield before the fighting ended. By law and tradition dating back to the Revolution, they had three ways to get there — through the Regular Army, the enrolled militia, or a volunteer unit.

A Federal Army recruit strikes a bold pose with pistol and flag in this *carte de visite*. Enlistment fever ran high early in the War. Men on both sides feared that the conflict would end before they got a chance to fight.

The United States Army was a force of professionals, led for the most part by West Point graduates and manned by those who were willing to enlist for five years. Because of the deep national distrust of standing armies, which dated from colonial times, the Regular Army had always been a meager force. On the eve of the Civil War, it had a total enlisted strength of 16,000 men — barely enough, as one observer noted, to police New York City. When the country split in two after the fall of Fort Sumter, its standing army was divided as well, with 30 per cent of its officers going South. President Lincoln called for the recruitment of an additional 22,700 Regular Army troops, but even at a time when the Union was consumed by patriotic fervor, Federal recruitment officers barely succeeded in signing up 2,000 men. And at no time during the War did the professional army reach its modest goal of 42,000 troops.

At the beginning of the War, the Confederate Congress provided for the creation of its own army of 10,000 men, but professional soldiers remained only a small minority in the South as well as the North. One reason for this was that Americans held it as an article of faith that patriotic amateurs made better troops than did paid professionals. The belief was grounded in tradition: The Revolutionary War had been fought and won by soldier-civilians who grasped their muskets and followed the leadership of amateur generals; in the War of 1812, Andrew Jackson and an outnumbered force of backwoodsmen had put to rout a great army of British veterans at the Battle of New Orleans; and it was largely the volunteers who had gained the victory in the Mexican War.

In theory, the backbone of the country's defense since Revolutionary times had been the enrolled militia. Every able-bodied male between the ages of 18 and 45 was required by law in most states to muster for drill once or twice a year. But by the middle of the century, increasing numbers of militiamen, for whom even one or two muster days a year had become a resented inconvenience, simply stayed away, paying or ignoring the fine for nonattendance that many states imposed but few enforced.

Between 1840 and 1851, seven states, including New York, abolished compulsory militia service entirely, and others eliminated the fine for absentees. Some of the frontier states never developed a militia system. The state militias that were preserved often formed the basis for home-guard units during the Civil War, operating within state boundaries.

Even as the compulsory militia system was waning, however, military-minded citizens continued to band together in amateur units. These volunteer militia companies, raised at private expense by local groups, had been in evidence since colonial times; the first to be organized, in 1638, was Boston's Ancient and Honorable Artillery Company. In the first half of the 19th Century, the volunteer companies had thrived during times of crisis. Great numbers of these volunteers had fought under U.S. Army authority during the Mexican War.

In peacetime, patriotic motives for membership gave way to more sociable impulses. Many of the older units became elitist clubs of 50 to 100 members who spent an inordinate amount of money and time acquiring splendid uniforms. The officers and men of the Detroit Light Guard, according to an armorer and musician employed by them in

1857, were "all gentlemen of wealth and prominence, who had joined the company just for the pleasure they would derive by being a soldier." Still, some of these units proved their usefulness as a peacetime police force, quelling riots and controlling mobs when called upon to do so.

As early as the 1820s, the old elitist companies had been joined by other, more proletarian volunteer units, many of which were composed entirely of immigrants. Some of these ethnic contingents — especially the Irish — met with ostracism and even violence from rival units. The Governors of Massachusetts and Connecticut went so far as to attempt to "disband all military companies of foreign birth." But such disputes were overshadowed — indeed, overwhelmed — by the events of 1861.

When the Federal and Confederate governments issued a call to arms, the existing volunteer militias responded en masse, and new units proliferated overnight. These volunteers were the bedrock of the Civil War armies. For the most part, they offered their services not to the central governments but to their states, which had always been the focus of their patriotism.

Although volunteer companies were under state jurisdiction, they still retained considerable leeway in matters of uniform, drill, armament and regulations. Initially, the enlistment period was relatively brief — three months in the North and one year in the South. Officers were generally elected, and since the units were locally formed, relatives, friends and neighbors could serve in the same company.

The volunteers were organized by the Governors of their states into regiments, consisting of 10 companies of approximately

100 men each, with the companies usually grouped according to region. Thus the Lynchburg Rifles became Company E of the 11th Virginia Infantry, and the Granite State Guards were renamed Company H, 2nd New Hampshire Volunteer Infantry. In addition, individual volunteers would be fed into the ranks to bring a new regiment up to full strength. The Governor appointed the senior officers, or simply confirmed those elected by the soldiers; he then transferred command of the regiments to the central government. Following a brief period of

These fresh-faced young Confederate militiamen were recruited by the 1st Virginia Infantry, whose battle flag appears above. Recruits exuded confidence when the War began. Wrote a foreign observer visiting the Confederacy in 1861: "Every private feels a determination, not only to carry his regiment through the fight, but to see his country through the War."

rudimentary basic training, the regiments joined others in the field, where they were organized into brigades, divisions and corps.

"Who will come up and sign the roll?" shouted the recruiting officers in the town squares, and young men rushed forward with all the zeal of repentant sinners at a backwoods revival meeting. The appeals to a man's patriotism and sense of honor were compelling, but there were other, less lofty reasons for enlisting in the Army. Standing back would have meant missing the excitement and glory, disappointing friends and community, and, even worse, risking the epithet of coward.

There was also the pay, a particularly meaningful factor in the North. Although a private in the Union Army would receive just $13 a month (for a Confederate it would be two dollars less), the North was suffering from widespread unemployment. Early in 1862, faced with declining enlistments, the Federal government authorized a $100 bounty for all volunteers. And as the War continued, many states paid even higher enlistment bonuses, some amounting to several hundred dollars. Such money was enticing to family men who could not find jobs. Enoch T. Baker, an enlistee from Pennsylvania, wrote to his wife: "It is no use for you to fret or cry about me, for you know if I could have got work I wood not have left you or the children."

In time, Baker and others would learn that army pay was not as regular as they had supposed. In the South, some men would go a year at a time without being paid, only to find Confederate currency so inflated that when their pay did come, it bought next to nothing.

Ultimately, the troops of both sides were sustained by other motives — patriotism, and the urge to punish the transgressor. "I did not come for money and good living," Private Samuel Croft of Pennsylvania wrote in 1861. He felt "proud and sanguine of success," knowing that the bayonets of his regiment were "in loyal hands that will plunge them deep in the hearts of those who have disgraced that flag which has protected them and us, their freedom and ours."

The preservation of the Union was the overriding goal of the foreign-born men who enlisted in the Federal Army. They had come to the United States for liberty and opportunity, and they did not intend to relinquish without a fight the form of government that they believed best represented those ideals. Philip Smith of the 8th Missouri, a German immigrant, wrote in his diary on the day after the defeat at Bull Run in 1861 that he had "grasped the weapon of death for the purpose of doing my part in defending and upholding the integrity, laws and the preservation of my adopted country from a band of contemptible traitors who would if they can accomplish their hellish designs, destroy the best and noblest government on earth."

For some Northerners, the War was a crusade to end slavery. "Slavery must die," wrote one Vermont corporal, "and if the South insists on being buried in the same grave I shall see in it nothing but the retributive hand of God." Some would even look upon the early years of Federal failure on the battlefield as God's punishment for temporizing on the issue of slavery for so long. Yet such sentiments were in the minority. Among the two million men who would wear the blue, few had any real interest in abolish-

Recruiting broadsides trumpet bellicose appeals for men to fill the ranks of the Federal and Confederate Armies. The organizers of new regiments often lured enlistees with the bait of extra money, fine weapons or special privileges — and then failed to make good on their promises.

WASHINGTON ARTILLERY
OF
NEW ORLEANS.
RECRUITS WANTED.

Officers of this Battalion are now in the South to enlist such Young Men, citizens of Louisiana, as are within conscript ages, who may come forward and offer themselves for service.

By special authority of the Secreta___ War, any person liable to conscriptio___ be enlisted, and conscripts enrolled m___ assigned to fill up this organization.

A bounty of FIFTY DOLLARS will be paid to all liable to co___ who come properly recommended.

The recruiting stations will be Mobile, Ala.; Jackson, Miss.; and o___ on the N. O. J. & G. N. R. Road, nearer New Orleans.

Captain M. B. MILLER, 3d Company, will be stationed at Mobi___ cruiting Officer; and Captain SQUIRES, 1st Company; Captain RICH___ Company, and Lieut. NORCOM, 4th Company, at Jackson, and vicinity___ or to the undersigned, at Mobile, applications may be addressed.

J. B. WALTON___
Col. Com'g and Chief of Artillery, 1st Army Corps, De___

I have established my Recruiting Office at Room No. 82, Bown___ Jackson, Miss.

C. W. SQUIRE___

HOME GUARDS!
To Arms! To Arms!
YOUR CAPITOL IS IN DANGER!

"It is expected that this Company will in all of to-morrow enlist for THREE MONTHS SERVICE, as they are NOW WANTED for the defense of Washington AT ONCE, and ought to be ready to take the Cars for Portland Wednesday morning, or Thursday at latest J. L. HODGDON, Ass't Gen'l.

PURSUANT TO THE FOREGOING REQUEST, THE

SKOWHEGAN DRILL CLUB,

And our PATRIOTIC CITIZENS generally, are requested to meet at

RALLY ROUND
THE FLAG, BOYS!
100 MEN WANTED!!
For the 23d Mich. Infantry.

Enlist before April 1st, secure the Government Bounty of $300 00,

AND "KEEP OUT OF THE DRAFT!"

Government Bounty, $300; State Bounty, $100; Town Bounty, $100.

Apply to WM. SICKELS, St. Johns, o___

EXCURSION PARTY
FOR THE
SUNNY SOUTH!

1776!   **1862!**

NINE MONTHS' Volunteers Received up t___

the 16th instant, for the Second and Eighth Michigan Regiments and for a new company of Sharp Shooters.

0th of December find you still EXPOSED TO THE DRAF___

___General Recruiting Office, No. 8 Noble's Block, BATTLE CREEK, and enlist. Choice of R___ ___as far as practical.

___is filled by the 30th, the Draft will certainly be made.

CAPT. C. BYINGTON and **LIEUT. J. G. SMITH.**
___yle Creek, Mich.
RECRUITING OFFICER___

REGIMENT ORDERED SOUTH!

National Guards
COL. P. LYLE
RECRUITS WANTED!
AT THE ARMORY.
RAC___ ___XTH

Rekruten Verlangt

für das

26. Regiment
Wisc. Volunteers!!

Ver. Staaten Bount___ aus dem Dienst en___ **$302** für ___

27 Dollars und eine Mona___ bezahlt, wenn die Mannschaft___ Löhnung und Verpflegung beg___

Jeder Deutscher fü___ mente anschließen.

Rekrutirungs-Office: Vier___ Halle, an Ostwasserstraße, 7.

FIRE ZOUAVES!
Company F,
RECRUITS WANTED!

Who will be Mustered in, Equipped and sent to Camp Immediately!

PAY AND RATIONS TO COMMENCE AT ONCE!
CENTRAL HEAD QUARTERS
No. 403 Walnut

ROLLS ALSO OPEN AT THE HOUSES OF THE FOLLOW___ GLOBE ENGINE CO. Germantown Road, ___ INDEPENDENCE HOSE George St. belo___

9th Regiment.
ON TO WASHINGTON!
DOWN WITH THE
REBELLION!
GREEN MOUNTAIN BOYS AWAKE!

I am authorized to recruit for the 9th Regiment of Infantry of Vt. Volunteers. A company is wanted in Caledonia County in 10 days.

Term of Enlistment three years, unless sooner discharged. Pay $23.25 per month and rations.

COME TO THE RESCUE OF OUR GLORIOUS REPUBLIC!

Call at my Office in this Village and information will be given and enlistments made.

___cer.

Mounted Rangers!

TERRY AND LUBBOCK'S REGIMENT!
FOR VIRGINIA DURING THE WAR!!

A company of not less than 64 nor more than 100 privates, is now being organized for the above service.

Each man must furnish the equipments for his horse, and arm himself, either with a short rifle or double barrell shot gun, and a six-shooter. Transportation from Alleyton to Virginia free! The best horses are now being purchased and will be furnished to the men in Virginia.

The undersigned is now ready to enlist men and will return to LaGrange on Saturday the 24th inst.

A roll will be left at the office of Fred Tate, Esq., to whom application may be made during my absence.

LOUIS M. STROBEL,
Enrolling officer.

HIBERNIA GREENS
IN THE
IRISH BRIGADE.

COL. THOS. FRANCIS MEAGHER & LIEUT. COL. NUGENT,
OF THE NEW YORK
SIXTY-NINTH REGIMENT,

To recruit a Company to be attached to the Irish Brigade under the Gallant Gen. Shields. We call upon all Patriotic Irishmen to enroll themselves for this Brigade.

Recruiting Station, Hibernia Greens' Armory,
Military Hall, Library Street.

RICHARD DILLON, 1st Lieutenant.
PETER CONLIN, 2d Lieutenant.

JOHN P. DUNNE,
CAPTAIN.

ing slavery. For every Federal who voiced his sympathy for the plight of the slaves, there was a legion who felt nothing but indifference or outright hostility.

Just as most Northerners did not fight to end slavery, most Southerners did not fight to preserve it. By and large, owning slaves was the privilege of the well-to-do. The rank and file of the Southern armies was composed of farmers and laborers who volunteered to protect home and everything dear from Northern invaders, to keep their traditions and to be left alone. Many believed that the Federal government was in the hands of a band of tyrannical, law-breaking fanatics who were bent on destroying not only the South but the Constitution and states' rights as well.

The Confederate cause was as holy to Southerners as the American Revolution had been to their forefathers. "I believe," wrote Sergeant John Hagan of Georgia, "we will have to fight like Washington did, but I hope our people will never be reduced to destress & poverty as the people of that day was, but if nothing else will give us our liberties I am willing for the time to come."

For all of their perceived differences, the Northerners and Southerners who rushed to take up arms had much in common. Most of the volunteers on both sides brought with them the language, ideas and customs of rural America. Nearly half of the men who donned the blue had been farmers, and almost two thirds of the Confederate recruits traded the plow for the gun. The remainder entered the service from any of a multitude of trades: More than 300 different occupations were represented in the Federal Army, and more than 100 in the Confederate.

Especially in the North, the wide range of vocations represented in the ranks of any sizable outfit made for a remarkable versatility in the field. When a weapon or piece of equipment was in need of repair, there was usually someone near at hand who knew how to fix it. Experienced workers were found to repair railroads, improvise bridges and construct winter camps. The South would suffer somewhat because of a lesser degree of diversity: A number of Confederate recruits listed their prewar occupation simply as "gentleman."

The majority of the soldiers on both sides were white, native-born, Protestant, unmarried — and young. The minimum age for enlistment on either side was 18, and four out of five men in both Armies were between that age and 29. Many of the rest were even younger. Boys eager to get into the fray, but unwilling to lie outright, often wrote the numeral 18 on slips of paper, which they then placed inside their shoes. When a recruiting officer asked how old they were, they could respond truthfully, "I'm over 18." Such punctiliousness was often unnecessary, because a number of recruiters simply ignored age regulations. And for musicians and drummer boys there were no such restrictions; Private Edward Black, for example, joined the 21st Indiana as a musician at the age of nine.

Those who were determined to serve the cause in spite of their age were not all youngsters. A member of Virginia's Richmond Howitzers recalled that he had known personally "six men over sixty years who volunteered, and served in the ranks, throughout the war." In North Carolina, in July 1862, one E. Pollard gave his age as 62 when he joined the 5th North Carolina Infantry, al-

Women Who Wore the Blue and the Gray

Not all of the soldiers who fought in the blue and the gray were men. Adventure-seeking women — perhaps as many as several hundred — disguised themselves as males and took up arms. Although the true identity of most was quickly discovered, some managed to sustain the deception for months and even years.

Sara Edmonds, a Canadian immigrant who joined the 2nd Michigan Infantry in 1861 under the name of Frank Thompson, was a master of disguise. In her account of her war experiences, she related that General George B. McClellan employed her as a spy during the Peninsular Campaign in 1862 — completely unaware of Private Thompson's true identity. For her first mission, she blackened her face with silver nitrate, covered her hair with a wig and slipped behind Confederate lines at Yorktown dressed as a young male slave.

On other occasions Edmonds posed as a female slave, a dry-goods clerk and a Confederate infantryman, infiltrating enemy lines 11 times in all without detection. In 1863 she contracted malaria, and rather than submit to a medical examination that might reveal her gender, she deserted and resumed civilian life as a woman. Not until 1883 did she confess her secret life as a soldier.

Even more remarkable was the career of Jennie Hodgers, an Irish woman who enlisted under the alias of Albert Cashier in the 95th Illinois Volunteers. Described by a fellow soldier as "the smallest man in the company," she fought at Vicksburg, in the Red River Campaign and at Nashville before being mustered out in 1865. After the War, she kept her masculine identity and even collected a soldier's pension. Not until 1911, when an automobile accident forced her hospitalization for surgery, was her true identity uncovered. When the Bureau of Pensions convened hearings to determine whether to continue her government stipend, her wartime comrades testified in her behalf. The board ruled that Hodgers was indeed a veteran, entitled to all the benefits thereof.

Frances Clalin, who adopted a masculine identity in order to fight with the Federals in Missouri, appears in feminine dress and in the uniform of a state militia cavalryman.

though he was probably over 70; he was soon discharged, because rheumatism prevented him from performing his soldierly duties. But he was not the oldest soldier of the War. That distinction went to Curtis King, who enlisted in the 37th Iowa Infantry in November 1862 at the age of 80. King served nearly six months before being discharged for disability. His regiment, which was nicknamed the Graybeards, had 145 soldiers aged 60 or older.

The average Civil War soldier stood between five feet five inches and five feet nine, but there is no evidence that height, or the lack of it, kept anyone from the War who wanted to go. The shortest Federal soldier on record had to hustle to keep up with his comrades in the 192nd Ohio Infantry; he was just three feet four inches from boot sole to kepi.

It would have taken two of him, stacked end on end, to approach the stature of Captain David Van Buskirk of the 27th Indiana Infantry, who stood just one inch short of seven feet — the loftiest pinnacle in a 100-man company that boasted 80 men above six feet. When the 380-pound Van Buskirk was captured in 1862 and sent to a Richmond prison, he agreed to let a Southern entrepreneur put him on exhibit as "the biggest Yankee in the world." Even President Jefferson Davis came to see him, and was astounded by the mischievous Van Buskirk's claim that when his six sisters bade him farewell back home in Bloomington, Indiana, they "leaned down and kissed me on top of my head."

Military units were made even more diverse by the intermingling of recruits from different regions — and different nations. Company H of the 8th Michigan, for example, had only 37 Michiganders in its

The 69th New York State Militia, a regiment of Irishmen, marches past St. Patrick's Cathedral in Manhattan before departing for Washington, D.C., in April 1861. The regiment suffered the loss of 45 officers and men at the First Battle of Bull Run.

ranks; the remainder comprised 47 New Yorkers, 26 Americans from other states, seven Canadians, five Englishmen, four Germans, two Irishmen, one Scotsman, one Dutchman and one mysterious individual who listed as his nationality "the ocean." Because of such mixtures, many camps were a babel of tongues; one Federal colonel, it was reported, had to issue his orders in seven languages.

Many of these immigrants had come to the United States as refugees from the Irish potato famine and the European revolutionary upheavals of the 1840s. Most of them had settled in the North, where wage work was then abundant and land cheap. By 1860 nearly a third of the North's male population was foreign-born, and almost one in every four Union soldiers was a first-generation American. President Lincoln gave general's commissions to well-known European political expatriates — such as the Germans Franz Sigel and Carl Schurz, the Frenchman Regis de Trobriand, the Irishman Thomas Meagher — as an inducement to their fellow immigrants to enlist under their banners.

More than 200,000 Germans served in the Northern armies, and scores of regiments had German majorities. The 9th Wisconsin had only a few non-Germans in its ranks; New York and Ohio furnished 16 regiments that were almost totally German in make-up. "I goes to fight mit Sigel," many of these soldiers sang as they marched off to war, only to find that their beloved general and countryman was an incompetent who got a good many of them needlessly killed.

The ranks of the Union armies were bolstered by other large groups of foreign-born volunteers, including 50,000 Englishmen, 50,000 Canadians and 150,000 Irishmen. The Irish alone constituted the majority of at least 20 Federal regiments. French residents of New York City manned and equipped the 55th New York, dubbing it "La Garde Lafayette." The 15th Wisconsin was all Scandinavian; one company alone had five men named Ole Olsen, and in the regiment as a whole there were more than 128 Oles of varying surnames. The 79th New York, composed principally of Scotsmen, wore kilts for full-dress ceremonies but donned more practical Tartan trousers when in the field.

Generally, the foreign-born soldiers were held in low esteem by their native-born comrades in arms, especially late in the War, when energetic recruiters began plying their trade at the gangplanks of ships just in from Europe, and even recruiting overseas. In 1864 the Union's Colonel Theodore Lyman, of General George G. Meade's staff, complained of "these gentlemen who would overwhelm us with Germans, negroes, and the offscourings of great cities." Compared with such common breeds, Lyman sneered, the Rebels, "in all their rags and squalor, are like wolf-hounds."

Yet some of those Rebel "wolf-hounds" were themselves immigrants. Though they never numbered more than 9 per cent of the Confederate forces, men from overseas made their presence felt in the ranks. Irish-born Patrick R. Cleburne of Arkansas rose to the rank of major general and proved to be one of the most capable Confederate commanders. There were Irish companies, Ger-

Federal Army recruiters enlist German and Irish immigrants fresh off the boat from Europe at Castle Garden in New York City. Nearly a fifth of the North's population was foreign-born when the War began, and some 500,000 immigrants served in the Federal Army.

George Washington, a Caddo Indian chief, was captain of an Indian unit that fought for the Confederacy. Indian troops on both sides acquitted themselves well in battle, but white officers occasionally complained about their penchant for scalping the fallen foe.

man companies and from Louisiana a mixed European battalion led by the resplendent Frenchman, Count Camille Armand Jules Marie, Prince de Polignac — simplified to "Polecat" by a Texas unit he commanded later. A company of Georgia mountaineers listened in open-mouthed wonder one day as the Prince shouted commands to a regiment in French. One of the Georgians called his speech "gibberish," and marveled that the men responded smartly, "jes' like he was talking sense!"

The muster rolls of North and South also included the names of American Indians. Perhaps 12,000 served the Confederacy, most of them members of the Five Civilized Tribes — Cherokee, Chickasaw, Choc-taw, Creek and Seminole — living out in the Indian Territory. Altogether, the Confederates would raise 11 regiments and seven independent battalions of Indians in the West, not to mention the few hundred Indians who were scattered through some of the white regiments from North Carolina, Tennessee and Kentucky.

Most Indian soldiers wore uniforms or conventional civilian clothing, with such additional adornments as silver earrings and feathered headbands. The attire of some of the frontier Indians was even more colorful: "Their faces were painted, and their long straight hair, tied in a queue, hung down behind," wrote a Missouri Confederate. "Their dress was chiefly in the Indian costume — buckskin hunting-shirts, dyed of almost every color, leggings, and moccasins of the same material, with little bells, rattles, ear-rings, and similar paraphernalia. Many of them were bareheaded and about half carried only bows and arrows, tomahawks, and war-clubs."

Ill-treated and ignored even by some of their own officers, many Indian Confederates had little heart for the Southern cause. Much the same could be said of the 3,500 or more Indians who wore the blue. Frequently they were enlisted merely to take advantage of old tribal hatreds and pit Union Indian against Confederate Indian.

The Federal commanders demonstrated little more regard for the few hundred Mexican-Americans who took up arms, primarily in regiments from Colorado, New Mexico and Texas. As a result, many of these troops deserted or even went over to the other side during the War.

The continent's largest minority — the Negro — had a particularly difficult time be-

coming a soldier, let alone proving himself. At the War's outset, the North was reluctant to put blacks in uniform. White civilians and soldiers alike argued strenuously against it. Enlisting blacks would degrade the Federal Army and be an open incitement for rebellion, they claimed. More important, it would threaten white supremacy. "The Southern people are rebels to the government," wrote an enlisted man of the 110th Pennsylvania, "but thay are White and God never intended a nigger to put white people Down."

Blacks were widely regarded as an inferior race, with whom thousands of Yanks vowed they would not serve. Yet Northern abolitionists and humanitarians argued that the use of Negro troops would bring a speedy

end to the War and teach black men skills and disciplines they would need in postwar society. "Give them a chance," the eloquent ex-slave Frederick Douglass pleaded. "I don't say that they will fight better than other men. All I say is, give them a chance!" But the issue was politically explosive, especially in those slave states still loyal to the Union, such as Missouri and Kentucky, and both President Lincoln and Congress moved cautiously.

Then, in the summer of 1862, Congress — facing a shortage of troops — passed the Confiscation Act, which authorized the President to use escaped slaves in the suppression of the rebellion. Furthermore, Congress enacted legislation permitting the drafting of blacks for "any military or naval

Black artillerymen recruited by the Federals from among former slaves in Tennessee drill at their weapon in 1864. Commanded by white officers, this unit, Battery A of the 2nd U.S. Colored Light Artillery, helped man the Union defenses during the Battle of Nashville.

service for which they may be found competent." Armed with these new laws, Lincoln authorized the full-scale recruitment of black soldiers late in 1862.

Once mustered into the service, blacks faced discrimination of every kind. Most white soldiers thought them lazy and insolent, and many resented them as the cause of the War. "I have slept on the soft side of a board, in the mud, and every other place that was lousy and dirty," grumbled Private Richard Puffer of the 8th Illinois Infantry. "I have drank out of goose ponds, horse tracks, etc., for the last eighteen months, all for the poor nigger; and I have yet to see the first one that I think has been benefitted by it."

Although black units did more than their share of menial tasks, some whites persisted in the belief that blacks were coddled by

Two black infantrymen sit for their portrait shortly after enlisting in the Federal Army. By August 1863, there were 14 black regiments serving with the Federal Army and 24 more in the process of formation.

the authorities. After a day of shoveling mud, one New Hampshire soldier griped that "some of the boys say that the Army Moto is First the Negro, then the mule, then the white man."

Opposition was slow in dying, but as the sight of blacks in uniform became more and more commonplace, they were gradually accepted as soldiers—although rarely as equals. Whites appreciated having blacks available to relieve them of such onerous duties as building fortifications and roads. And ambitious young officers—both commissioned and noncommissioned—found that they could attain higher rank in black regiments. Here and there, individual acts of decency gave rise to a tentative spirit of comradeship. Some white Federals took it upon themselves to teach black soldiers to read and write, and even welcomed the blacks to their church services. A few black officers were commissioned in state regiments, but the Federal War Department did not assent to such appointments until the last year of the War. And not until 1864 would the black soldier finally receive the same pay as his white counterpart.

What changed the attitude of white soldiers and civilians more than anything else was the black man's performance in battle. During the last three years of the War, black Federal regiments participated in more than 33 major battles. Out in the Indian Territory in 1863, Major General James G. Blunt had a black regiment among his troops when he met the enemy at Honey Springs. After the battle, in which the 1st Kansas Colored Volunteers distinguished themselves, General Blunt declared: "Their coolness and bravery I have never seen surpassed; they were in the hottest of the fight, and opposed to Texas

Headed by its regimental band, the 73rd Ohio Infantry forms up to march through downtown Chillicothe on its departure for western Virginia in 1862. The unit subsequently fought in the Shenandoah Valley, at the Second Battle of Bull Run and at Gettysburg, losing by the War's end a third of its nearly 1,000 officers and men.

troops twice their number, whom they completely routed."

Altogether, 178,892 blacks served in the Union Army, and 32,369, or more than a sixth of their number, died in uniform—a slightly higher proportion than among their white comrades. The Federal government awarded at least 21 black soldiers its newly created Medal of Honor.

At first, the Confederate government did not recognize blacks in the Federal Army as legitimate soldiers. Official policy, approved by Jefferson Davis himself, condemned Federal white officers of black regiments to execution—for leading a "servile insurrection." And the unofficial policy of many Confederate soldiers was to take no black prisoners. Many Southerners reacted with particular fury when confronted with ex-slaves carrying weapons against them. During the last two years of the conflict, a number of massacres of black soldiers were reported. Some of the accounts were much exaggerated, but there is no doubt that captured, wounded and often unarmed black soldiers—at Fort Pillow in Tennessee, Poison Spring in Arkansas and Saltville in Virginia—were murdered by wrathful Confederates.

Not surprisingly, the proposal that blacks be mobilized for military service proved even more explosive in the Confederacy than in the Union. The Confederacy had an enormous manpower reserve in the 3.5 million slaves and 132,000 free blacks in the South in 1861. Some slaves felt great loyalty to their masters and asked to be allowed to take up arms to defend what was, after all, their homeland too.

Many did go to war for the Confederacy as cooks, servants, musicians and teamsters, occasionally even performing picket duty. At times, one of them would grasp a fallen weapon in the heat of battle and join the fight, but such heroic lapses were frowned upon. The apprehension that arming slaves would invite insurrection was widespread in the South. And beyond that fear lay the uneasy conviction that accepting Negroes as soldiers—the most noble of callings in the view of many Southerners—posed a mortal threat to the assumptions of white superiority.

Debate on the question within the South was long and bitter. Finally, in March 1865, confronted with a desperate shortage of fighting men, the Confederate Congress by a slim majority passed legislation calling for the enlistment of 300,000 black soldiers. But the War ended before the few blacks enrolled under the act could see combat.

The War's appetite for human fodder proved to be voracious, and after the initial rush of patriotism waned, fewer and fewer volunteers stepped forward. To fill their depleted ranks, both sides were compelled to adopt conscription—the Confederacy in 1862 and the Union a year later—and thenceforth the quality of the regiments would generally decline.

The practice of substitution did nothing to maintain standards. Both sides had provisions allowing a conscript to send another man to serve in his stead. In some cases, the rule worked to the good. A family, for example, might send a younger man as a substitute for an important breadwinner.

It was the hiring of substitutes, however, that bred much discontent, since it blatantly favored the wealthier classes. A Southern farmer might have to raise as much as $6,000

The 1st Louisiana Zouave Battalion, a flamboyant unit composed mainly of French-speaking men from New Orleans, drills at Pensacola, Florida, in 1862. According to a newspaper account, the troops were "generally small, but wiry, muscular, active as cats and brown as a side of sole leather."

in his inflated currency to hire a substitute. Yet in 1863, Confederate Secretary of War James Seddon estimated that more than 50,000 Southerners had bought their way out of military service in this fashion. When the supply of able-bodied substitutes for hire had been exhausted, the recruitment brokers turned to the sick and the weak.

In the North, the number of substitutes rose as high as 118,000. Medical officers in the field were horrified to discover new recruits arriving with crippled limbs, incurable diseases and severe mental deficiencies. Of 57 replacements dispatched to a New York artillery outfit in 1863 and 1864, one third were rejected as completely unfit for service. There was a widely circulated report that one recruitment broker had lured an inmate away from a New York mental asylum and foisted him on the Army as a substitute.

A provision in the North that enabled a conscript to buy his way out of the Army with cold cash provoked deep public resentment. The commutation fee was $300, a sum that working men could scarcely afford, and the public outcry against the practice forced its abandonment.

The draft provisions drastically altered the composition of the Armies, and veteran soldiers on both sides voiced their disgust; Frank Wilkeson, a New York artilleryman, characterized the recruits supplied to the Federal Army late in the War as "the scum of the slums." Fortunately for the units they joined, a fair number of these newcomers deserted shortly after their arrival, especially the bounty jumpers, who enlisted under assumed names to obtain bonuses, then deserted to enlist yet again under another name.

By the time the War was in its final months, many once-proud regiments had been reduced to mere shadows by death, disease, desertion and expired terms of service. Most of the conscripts and bounty men who remained with their units lacked the determination and experience of their predecessors in battle.

Still, the shortcomings of the recruits only stiffened the resolve of some veterans to stay the course. "If new men won't finish the job, old men must," wrote Benjamin F. Falls of the 19th Massachusetts when he, like thousands of other soldiers whose devotion to cause and duty remained high, reenlisted early in 1864. "As long as Uncle Sam wants a man, here's Ben Falls." Such was the testimony of the stalwarts: Having started something, they would "finish the job." But in the case of Ben Falls, there would be one patriot less when the task was done. Four months after reenlisting, he died in battle at Spotsylvania.

A Craving for Family Portraits

Beginning with the first call to arms, thousands of soldiers and their families sat for the local photographer. Although photography was barely 30 years old, technical advances in the art — primarily a process that yielded inexpensive paper prints — made it possible for ordinary Americans to have their portraits taken. Soldiers were eager to pose in uniform with their loved ones; they sensed that the War would be the climactic event in their lives, and they meant to leave a record of their participation. So popular were the wartime portraits that poet and essayist Dr. Oliver Wendell Holmes called them "the social currency, the sentimental greenbacks of civilization."

DR. HUGH WYTHE DAVIS, C.S.A.
MEDICAL STAFF, AND WIFE MARY

SERGEANT JOEL S. STEVENS, 16TH MAINE INFANTRY, AND FAMILY

COLONEL VANNOY H. MANNING,
3RD ARKANSAS, C.S.A., AND WIFE

VIRGINIA SOLDIER WITH
SISTER AND BROTHER

FEDERAL LIEUTENANT AND CHILD

SOLDIER OF THE 10TH CONNECTICUT AND RELATIVE

CONFEDERATE SOLDIER
R. B. CHAFFIN AND WIFE

UNION CORPORAL AND FAMILY

SERGEANT HENRY H. WAUGH, 12TH
MASSACHUSETTS INFANTRY, AND WIFE

FEDERAL SOLDIER WITH
BROTHER AND SISTERS

PENNSYLVANIA LIEUTENANT
F.L.O. ROEHRIG AND SON

NEW YORK CORPORAL AND WIFE

TEXAS PRIVATE AND WIFE

PRIVATE HENRY DIKEMAN, 53RD
NEW YORK, WITH FAMILY MEMBERS

41

CONFEDERATE SOLDIER AND
HIS TWO SISTERS

PRIVATE JOHN PICKLE,
18TH TEXAS CAVALRY, AND WIFE

CONFEDERATE COLONEL
AND WIFE

FEDERAL SERGEANT
AND WIFE

VERMONT CORPORAL AND FAMILY

ZOUAVE PRIVATE, 95TH PENNSYLVANIA, AND WIFE

CONNECTICUT PRIVATE
WILLIAM OATLEY AND WIFE

VERMONT ENLISTED MAN
AND WIFE

LIEUTENANT GEORGE K. BRADY,
14TH U.S. INFANTRY, AND WIFE

43

Camp Days

In March of 1862 the recently recruited 12th Connecticut Volunteers landed on Ship Island in the Gulf of Mexico to take part in the Federal expedition against New Orleans. As they marched through a city of tents, they passed the smartly saluting and tightly disciplined veterans of the 9th Connecticut and 26th Massachusetts. "Our greenhorns stared at them with a mixture of wonder, envy and gloomy foreboding," recalled the novelist John William De Forest, himself a greenhorn captain in the 12th. " 'Has it come to this!' they seemed to be thinking. 'Are freeborn Americans to be made slaves of in this fashion! And yet, what if those men should whip the Rebels, and we should run away!' "

The same emotions — wonder, envy, foreboding — were familiar to thousands of volunteers, both North and South, as they joined the armies in the field. These recruits had barely been introduced to military life in training camps back home. Could they adjust to the constraints of this life? Would they ever snap off salutes like veterans? Could they somehow find, in this strange city of tents, the courage to face the enemy's fire?

The camp was the place where the new soldier ceased to be a civilian and learned to become a soldier. Here his life would move to the rhythm of bugle and drum. Here he would learn discipline, hone his skills at drill, and experience the army's mysterious organization and chain of command. Pre-

sumably, he would become proficient in the handling of arms and care of his equipment. He would stand guard, in darkness and foul weather. He would learn how to pitch and strike a tent, how to kindle a fire in the field, and how to make the best of his strange new outdoor life, picking up the old soldier's tricks for securing rude comfort. If he was thrown into battle before he could absorb these lessons — which was often the case — he would at least have some sense of himself as an integral part of a machine, moving to the voice of command.

Within the narrow boundaries of the camp, the novice soldier would encounter a wider variety of human nature than he had ever been exposed to before. Sometimes he would be appalled: "I had no idea of the filth and vulgarity of men in camp," lamented a Mississippi volunteer. But for the most part he would get along. If he had any personal goal beyond survival, it was perhaps that attained by Captain Oliver Wendell Holmes Jr. of Massachusetts, who wrote to his father: "I started in this thing a boy; I am now a man."

Physically, the world the volunteer entered was enough to quell anyone's appetite for the military life. Throughout the War, the opposing armies tended to retrace or cross previous routes of march as they campaigned; thus all too often troops would camp in places that had held bivouacs before. The old campgrounds, with their accumulation of

REGULATIONS FOR
CAMP DEFIANCE

Reveille at	-	-	-	-	5
Breakfast Call at -	-	-	-		7
Guard Mounting at	-	-	-		9½
Dinner Call at	-	-	-		12
Company Drills from -	-	-		1 to 3
Dress Parade at	-	-	-	-	6
Tattoo at	-	-	-	-	9
Taps at					10

1. All non-commissioned Officers will be within the Camp at 8 P. M.

2. No commissioned Officer will be allowed to remain out of the Camp after Tattoo, without the permission of his Battalion Commander.

3. After 8 P. M. no loud singing, no cheering or firing arms will be allowed, nor any firing or cheering on the Sabbath. The Commandant requests that the troops will observe the Sabbath in an orderly and Christian-like manner.

4. Citizens visiting the Camp must obtain a written pass from Head Quarters.

5. Guards, when recognizing Staff Officers and commissioned Officers of the line, will pass them, in the daylight, without the countersign.

The Commandant will hold the various commanders strictly accountable to the observance of the above.

By order of   B. M. PRENTISS, Commandant.

ruined structures, stripped vegetation and heaps of garbage, were always uninviting and often dangerously unsanitary. Even at new campsites, the presence of thousands of men rapidly overtaxed the land. In wet weather, the ground was converted to quagmire. A disgusted Michigan recruit wrote home that he was being trained in a camp that was little better than "a wallow-hole," trampled by thousands of men into "a vast sea of mud." Confederates fared no better. A camp near Manassas, wrote a Virginia soldier, was "literally a lake of mud," with ground "so soft that you have to hold your breath to keep from sinking." Any visitor, he added, would be "perplexed whether to laugh or sympathize."

In summer the mud turned to dust. Moving about camp in hot weather, remarked a Connecticut infantryman, was like tramping through an ash heap: "One's mouth will be so full of dust that you do not want your teeth to touch one another." If a grasshopper jumped, observed an artilleryman wryly, it raised such a cloud of dust that the Confederates thought the Federal Army was on the move.

In this inhospitable terrain, the new soldiers pitched tents that would be their homes spring, summer and fall. Both sides initially favored the Sibley tent, named for its inventor, Henry H. Sibley, who later became a Confederate brigadier general. A large cone of canvas, 18 feet in diameter, 12 feet tall and supported by a center pole, the tent had a circular opening at the top for ventilation, and a cone-shaped stove for heat. It was comfortable for a dozen men, but regulations authorized up to 20: They slept in wheel-spoke fashion with their feet at the center. On cold or rainy days, with the tent flaps closed, the atmosphere inside could become intolerable. A Massachusetts artilleryman, John D. Billings, declared that to enter a Sibley on a rainy morning "and encounter the night's accumulation of nauseating exhalations from the bodies of twelve men (differing widely in their habits of personal cleanliness) was an experience which no old soldier has ever been known to recall with great enthusiasm."

In time, the Sibley was replaced with smaller, simpler tents. In the Federal armies the old wedge tent reappeared, really nothing more than a six-foot length of canvas draped over a horizontal ridgepole and staked to the ground at the sides. Flaps closed off the ends, giving the four to six men inside some privacy. But with only about seven square feet of space per man, sleeping was a cramped exercise. Even smaller was the dog tent—so called, observed a Federal soldier, because "it would only comfortably accommodate a dog, and a small one at that.'' Every soldier carried half of the tent with him. Two together would button their halves, drape them over an improvised ridgepole or stretch them between two trees, and then share the miserly interior with no end flaps to keep out wind or cold. The Confederates sometimes employed similar tents, but because of a perennial shortage of canvas, they often had to make do with crude ''shebangs,'' fashioned of brush and oilcloths arranged over a framework of poles.

Devising shelter in winter called for extra effort and ingenuity. Armed with axes and saws, men spread out in all directions, virtually denuding the landscape of trees. Sometimes genuine log cabins went up, but more frequently winter quarters were an amalgam of dirt, logs and whatever roofing materials came to hand. Men dug the floor down a foot or more below the surface, then laid logs around the perimeter to a height of about four feet and chinked them with mud. The roofs might be made of boards, thatch or shingles — or simply of canvas that was draped over a ridgepole and covered with oilcloth ground sheets or ponchos to help keep out the rain.

Many winter huts had fireplaces of sticks

daubed with mud, with a barrel for a chimney, and floors of barrel staves. Boxes and log ends made good stools to set before the crates that served as tables. Bayonets driven into the walls became candlesticks.

Army regulations called for the camps to be laid out in a rigid grid pattern, with officers' quarters at the front of each street and enlisted men's quarters aligned to the rear. Regulations spelled out the width of the camp's streets, the location of its kitchens and sinks, where the baggage trains should be parked, how far in front of the camp the pickets should be posted. Nothing was left to chance.

But often a lack of time or rough terrain made it impractical to adhere to the letter of the regulations. Many camps were laid out with "a hurly-burly lack of plan," artilleryman John Billings recalled. The rutted lanes that crisscrossed both summer and winter camps were assigned official names like Lincoln Avenue and Lee Boulevard— and unofficial ones such as Mud Lane and Starvation Alley.

Within the boundaries of these makeshift communities, the regiment quickly became the center of the new recruit's friendships and loyalties, and the source of his knowledge of Army operations.

In this composite photograph, supply wagons and troops move down planked streets as the 22nd Connecticut makes a sortie from winter camp at Miner's Hill, Virginia, in February 1863. What personal belongings could not fit in a knapsack had to be left behind.

At full strength, an infantry regiment was composed of 10 companies of about 100 men each. But once the fighting began and disease made inroads, regimental strength usually fell off sharply, sometimes to as low as 250 men. When the 1st Maine Heavy Artillery, which spent three years of the War on garrison duty in Washington, was reassigned to the Army of the Potomac, veterans watched in disbelief as it marched toward the battlefront at more than full strength. John Billings saw the endless column wind by one muggy May morning near Spotsylvania: " 'What regiment is this?' a bystander at the head of the column inquired. 'First Maine,' was the reply. After the columns had marched by a while, someone would again ask what regiment it was, only to find it still the First Maine." No veteran, added Billings, had ever dreamed of a fighting regiment that size.

Older regiments tended to be particularly small in the North, where the practice was to organize recruits into new regiments rather than send them to replace losses in veteran outfits. A new regiment would require a new set of officers, an opportunity for patronage that state Governors were rarely willing to forgo. In the Confederate armies, by contrast, depleted regiments were usually filled up with new recruits — a more effective arrangement that allowed green inductees to learn from veterans.

Union officers complained bitterly about their system, and attributed much of the enemy's early success to the Confederates' skill at training unseasoned troops. Captain John De Forest, observing the arrival in camp of a new regiment of Connecticut troops "as green as grass," wrote to his wife: "I need twenty men to fill up my company; and if I could draft them out of this regiment, they would be something like veterans in a fortnight; whereas it will take six months to bring them to the same point under their own raw officers and sergeants." He concluded derisively: "Why shouldn't even a politician understand that?"

The roster of a typical infantry company included a captain, one first and one second lieutenant, a first sergeant and four lower sergeants, eight corporals, two musicians, a wagoner and 82 privates. On both sides, volunteer units of some states had the privilege of electing their officers — which meant that a great many incompetents came to positions of command solely on the basis of their popularity or their electioneering skills. Many other unqualified men won posts of leadership through political patronage. De Forest told of a lieutenant in his regiment who was not only "a wretched officer," but also a coward. "Lieutenant Slick," as De Forest called him, once took an absence without leave and, on another occasion, fled a battle, leaving his troops to shift for themselves. Yet his luck held, and he remained in the service. Because of the man's extraordinary ability to survive, wrote De Forest, "the Twelfth still boasts the stupidest lieutenant in the brigade."

In an effort to weed out such undesirables, the Union and Confederate commands eventually abolished the election of officers and introduced boards of examinations for officer candidates. Experience, along with periodic reorganization on both sides, also helped to improve the quality of the officer corps. Nonetheless, there remained a number of political appointees who were not fit for command.

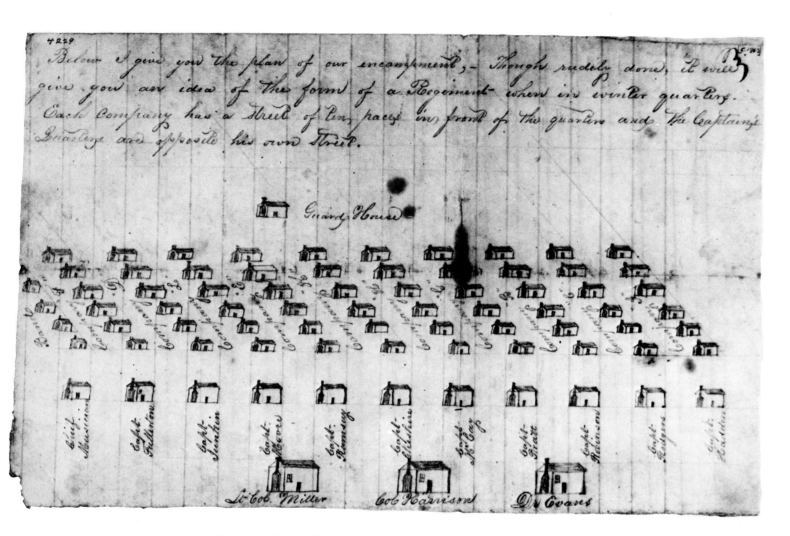

A soldier's meticulous rendering of the winter camp of the 1st South Carolina Rifles in Spotsylvania, Virginia, shows buildings arranged by company in neat rows, with captain's quarters at the head of each street. The artist sketched the camp on the back of a letter written in 1864.

Beyond the officers and men of his own company, the common soldier would know, by sight and reputation, the commissioned officers of his regiment, who included the colonel, lieutenant colonel, major, adjutant, quartermaster, surgeon, assistant surgeon and chaplain. He would certainly have some knowledge of the regiment's noncommissioned officers, especially the sergeant major, the quartermaster and the commissary sergeants.

But it was the first sergeant of a company, along with the noncommissioned officers under him, who dominated the soldier's life. They managed the day-to-day routine of the company — directing the men, keeping the roll, and handling the lowest level of the army's paper work.

The sergeants and corporals roused the men every morning. In both Union and Confederate camps, reveille was at 5 a.m. in the summer and 6 a.m. in the winter. It was not the time of day when men appeared at their best. Seeing Union troops turn out in the half-light of dawn, war correspondent George A. Townsend was struck by what a scruffy-looking lot they were: "Some wore one shoe, and others appeared shivering in their linen. They stood ludicrously in rank, and a succession of short, dry coughs ran up and down the line." The first sergeant took roll — the first of three roll calls held during the day — and passed the tally to a company officer. The camp was put into order, and breakfast eaten. About every two hours during the day, the company guard was changed. And throughout the day, the men drilled — in as many as five separate sessions, some lasting as long as two hours.

Private Oliver Norton of the 83rd Pennsylvania gave his impression of the routine:

Shelter for All Seasons

WALL TENT WITH FLAPS UP

LOG SHELTER

OFFICERS' LOG HOUSE

IMPORTED FRENCH BELL TENTS

Tents of all descriptions housed armies in warm weather and on the march. Winter quarters were more substantial but no less varied. Some men built shelters with palisaded walls and masonry chimneys, and a few even added front porches to provide a touch of home.

EY TENT

POLE-AND-THATCH HUT

GE TENT

WINTER WALL TENT

"The first thing in the morning is drill. Then drill, then drill again. Then drill, drill, a little more drill. Then drill, and lastly drill." Rarely did practice go beyond the regimental level, for the good reason that early in the War the officers, like their men, were almost all amateurs who lacked the skills to drill great numbers of men.

Generally, there was a regimental dress parade and inspection at the end of the afternoon. After supper at 6:30, those men not assigned to picket duty would have a stretch of free time to themselves before lights out at nine.

In the intervals between drills, the soldiers were kept busy with the arduous labors that maintained an army in the field: policing the camp, building roads or laying down pathways of pine logs, digging trenches for latrines, caring for horses and mules, repairing equipment. Supplies of wood, the primary fuel for heating and cooking, quickly became scarce near army encampments. Wood-cutting details might have to march several miles, stay for several days and employ a sizable wagon train to haul timber back to camp. The lack of potable water could be a problem, even when a regiment was encamped near a river or stream. Thousands of men and animals using the water quickly fouled the stream, and water parties might have to march along the banks for some distance to find drinkable water. Often, recalled artilleryman Billings, the best to be had was "only a warm, muddy, and stagnant fluid that had accumulated in some hollow."

For some recruits, the hard labor of army life came as a shock. Sixteen-year-old Private Elbridge Copp of the 3rd New Hampshire wrote of "men who at home were accus-tomed to nothing more strenuous than the handling of a yard stick and dry goods from over the counter, or light clerical work, lawyers, book keepers, school teachers, and among them were men of wealth, now finding themselves as privates in the ranks subject to the orders of superior officers, doing the work of porters and laborers in all kinds of necessary drudgery."

Although most men greeted their new circumstances without complaint, the sheer tedium of camp life soon took its toll. The days, observed a Mississippian, could be "one everlasting monotone: yesterday, today and tomorrow." Many recruits grew to despise the routine. "When this war is over I will whip the man that says 'fall in' to me," wrote a disgruntled Confederate. On both sides, malingerers became adept at "playing old soldier" — feigning illness at sick call — to win relief. There were even rare cases of men shooting themselves in the hand or foot to gain admission to the hospital.

For most fledgling officers, the first few weeks in camp were a nightmare of trying to master their new duties while concealing their ignorance from the troops. In many camps there were special night schools to enable officers to learn what they would be teaching the troops the next day. "Every night," wrote an Ohio sergeant, "I recite with the other 1st Sergts and 2nd Lieutenants. We shall finish Hardee's Tactics and then study the 'Army Regulations.' " Young Lieutenant Samuel A. Craig of the 105th Pennsylvania recalled spending a good deal of time during his first weeks in the Army sneaking off into the woods to shout commands to the trees.

But such stratagems rarely escaped the sharp eyes of the troops. Writing home about

Watercolor portraits of Confederate soldiers by artist William Ludwell Sheppard, a veteran of the War, portray typical uniforms of the three fighting branches of the Army. The artilleryman (left) was distinguished from the infantryman (center) by red trim on collar and cuffs; the cavalryman (right) wore yellow trim.

the "green officers" in camp, an Iowa soldier observed dryly: "It is rather a funny operation for one man to teach another what he don't know himself." The men of the 5th Wisconsin watched derisively as their raw colonel led his first regimental drill, lost his notes in the wind and dismissed the regiment in red-faced confusion. Of another bumbling colonel, a Pennsylvania infantryman wrote: "Col. Roberts has showed himself to be ignorant of the most simple company movements. We can only be justly called a mob & one not fit to face the enemy." Nor were the Confederates in much better shape. "Maneuvers of the most utterly impossible sort were taught to the men," recalled Virginia artilleryman George Eggleston. "Every

amateur officer had his own pet system."

Officers who were frank about their lack of experience got along better. Captain John Trice of the Confederate 4th Kentucky Infantry was esteemed by his men for his blunt reply to a superior's question about how he would deploy his troops when meeting the enemy: "Well, Major, I can't answer that according to the books, but I would risk myself with the Trigg County boys, and go in on main strength and awkwardness."

Both Armies attempted to maintain standards of performance among the officers and enlisted men by assigning a corps of inspectors general to monitor the condition of the regiments. An I.G., as such an officer was known, was empowered to mete out disci-

A company of the 40th Massachusetts stands at the guard during a bayonet drill at Miner's Hill, near Washington. For such drill, Federal troops used a French manual translated in 1852 by then-Captain George B. McClellan.

pline for infractions, and soldiers of all ranks respected his clout. Sergeant Thomas Livermore of the 5th New Hampshire described the preparations necessary to pass an I.G. inspection: "Every button must be in place and buttoned, every bit of metal polished bright, every gun as clean clear to the bottom of the bore as it could be made, every stitch sewed, every particle of dust absent, every strap in place, every man clean, every one's hair short and combed, every shoe blacked clear around the heels, every knapsack packed with a clean change of underclothes, and every cartridge, cap, and primer in its place."

In time, of course, the regimental officers learned their business, and the recruits began to turn into soldiers. When that happened, a mass drill became a wonderful sight to behold. Sergeant William Watson noted that steady drill gave the men of the 3rd Louisiana Infantry "soldierly bearing and military pride," and "brought them up to a high state of efficiency." He added: "The steadiness and regularity of their evolution in company or battalion drill would have done honor to any European troops."

Throughout the War, a soldier had little opportunity to spend extended periods of time away from the Army. Furloughs were seldom granted. Federal troops were often stationed too far from home to get much use from a furlough, and in the South, the troops were too few and too badly needed to be permitted generous leaves. Confederate General Daniel H. Hill once commented on the situation: "If our brave soldiers are not permitted to visit their homes, the next generation in the South will be composed of the descendants of skulkers and cowards."

55

Forced to remain in or near camp, soldiers on both sides filled their leisure hours with pastimes of their own devising. The tastes and off-duty behavior of some men were sufficiently seamy to shock tender young recruits newly arrived in camp. "There is some of the onerest men here that I ever saw," wrote Virginian Adam Radar, "and the most swearing and card playing and fitin and drunkenness that I ever saw at any place." An Illinois soldier told his family that "if there is any place on God's fair earth where wickedness 'stalketh abroad in daylight,' it is in the army."

Many young recruits feared corruption. "The majority of soldiers are a hard set," remarked an Iowa soldier. "They have every temptation to do wrong and if a man has not firmness enough he will soon be as bad as the worst." A Vermonter lamented that "I will be a perfect Barbarian if I Should Stay hear 3 years."

Men of strong religious convictions doubted that armies so depraved could succeed in battle. "One unceasing tide of blasphemy & wickedness, coarseness and obscenity," wrote a pious Mississippian. "Is it possible that God will bless a people as wicked as our soldiers? I fear not." Some generals tried to control the tide of scatalogical language, and the Union War Department even made swearing by officers an offense punishable at a dollar per oath. But the prohibition was largely ignored.

Hard language, combined with boredom and uncomfortably close quarters, led to quarrels — and the quarrels led to fights. In one camp, brawling was so prevalent that an Alabama soldier about to receive a visit from his civilian brother half-seriously advised him by mail to bring a shotgun to camp for

"A Wretched Class of Swindlers"

To the soldier in need of supplies, the sutler's tent offered a tantalizing bounty: tobacco, candy, tinned meats, shoelaces, patent medicines, fried pies, newspapers. But unscrupulous sutlers — a Dutch word meaning "to undertake low offices" — were legion, and often the soldier paid five times the true value of an item. Resentment of steep prices and often shoddy goods ran high in both Armies. A newspaper correspondent covering the War wrote that sutlers were "a wretched class of swindlers and well deserved all their troubles."

Their troubles were many indeed. Following armies on campaign, they risked being caught up in the action: At least one sutler was killed by stray fire. Yet their greatest problems came from irate customers. Midnight raids by soldiers on sutlers' tents were commonplace — and mostly overlooked by sympathetic officers. To avoid ruinous loss, sutlers sought to time the arrival of their wares with payday, and tried to sell out quickly.

As one soldier wrote, "The law recognized the sutler and the orders shielded him. That was theory. Everybody kicked and cursed him and plundered him. That was practice."

A group of sutlers pose with crates of their goods. Although these government-approved vendors occasionally advertised their wares *(left)*, such promotion was largely unnecessary, for the Army licensed only one sutler per post or regiment. To further ensure a captive clientele, many sutlers made change in scrip *(below)* negotiable only in the sutler's tent.

SAMUEL HATCH,
Sutler 7th Regiment,
O. V. M.
FIVE CENTS.

In a moment of whimsy, officers of the 3rd and 4th Pennsylvania Cavalry flourish whiskey bottles for an 1862 portrait captioned by the photographer "Illustrating the Hardships of War." Officers were allowed to buy whiskey, and many of them took full advantage of the privilege.

his own protection. Fights were particularly frequent when regiments of differing ethnic or national background were bivouacked together. Whites and blacks fought, and native-born Yankees fought with immigrant Germans. The Irish, it was widely believed, were ready to fight with anybody — a reputation that led to some fanciful tales. It was said of the 7th Missouri — the so-called Missouri Irish Brigade — that during its first day in camp, the 800 men on the roll were involved in no fewer than 900 fights. Describing the pugnacious 12th Connecticut, John De Forest explained to his wife that "many of my men are city toughs, in part Irish."

For all its sound and fury, brawling was not considered by the Army leadership to be nearly so damaging as another favored pas-

time, drinking whiskey. Army regulations prohibited the purchase of alcohol by enlisted men, and soldiers who violated the rule were punished. On those occasions when a soldier managed to beg or buy a bottle on the sly, he tended to drink it fast. Long dry spells and sudden binges formed the drinking pattern of the common soldier. "No one evil agent so much obstructs this army," Federal General George B. McClellan declared in 1862, "as the degrading vice of drunkenness." To eradicate drinking from the camps, he said, "would be worth 50,000 men to the armies of the United States." Confederate General Braxton Bragg concurred: "We have lost more valuable lives at the hands of the whiskey sellers than by the balls of our enemies."

To anybody familiar with camp life, the heavy drinking was easy enough to understand. "If you could look into our tents," wrote a Connecticut officer, "you would not wonder that consolation is sought for in whiskey. The never-ceasing rain streams at will through numerous rents and holes in the mouldy, rotten canvas. Nearly every night half the men are wet through while asleep unless they wake up, stack their clothing in the darkness, and sit on it with their rubber blankets over their heads, something not easy to do when they are so crowded that they can hardly move."

In the Union Army the men were occasionally treated to a small whiskey ration.

But a private in the ranks who wished to get additional whiskey from the commissary for medicinal purposes could do so only with a signed order. Soldiers on both sides found ways to skirt the rules, though. An enterprising man of the 2nd Tennessee smuggled whiskey into camp by pouring it into the barrel of his rifle. And members of a Mississippi company got a half gallon of whiskey past the camp guards by concealing it in a hollowed out watermelon; they then buried the melon beneath the floor of their tent and drank from it with a long straw.

Most men preferred not to know what was in their liquor. One Indiana officer wrote that he and his comrades drank a brew of

Risqué pictures printed on small cards offered teasing glimpses of the female form. Sutlers sold the cards to the troops for a quarter.

Entered according to Act of Congress, in the year 1864, by T. C. Vandermixer, in the clerk's office of the District Court for the District of Massachusetts.
GOT A BITE.
From the Original Drawing.

Entered according to Act of Congress, in the year 1864, by T. C. Vandermixer, in the clerk's office of the District Court for the District of Massachusetts.
THE ROSE OF THE BALLET.
From the Original Drawing.

Playing cards manufactured for Federal soldiers by a New York firm in 1862 feature four patriotic suits: Federal shields, five-pointed stars, flags and American eagles. Federal officers, along with Miss Liberty, adorn the face cards.

"bark juice, tar-water, turpentine, brown sugar, lamp-oil and alcohol." A Massachusetts cavalryman described his potion as "new and fiery, rough and nasty to take." The soldiers honored the stuff with such titles as "Old Red Eye," "Bust Skull," "Rifle Knock-Knee," "Oh, Be Joyful" and "Oil of Gladness."

Drunkenness in the officer corps was regarded as highly dangerous to morale and order. Unlike the enlisted men, the officers could get whiskey from the commissary when they wanted it — at a mere "31¢ per gallon," reported Private Alfred Davenport of the 5th New York. As a result, both Armies had far too many cases like that of the besotted Confederate staff officer at the Battle of Ball's Bluff who mistook a detachment of Federals for his own troops and directed them to attack Confederate positions.

Another favorite vice for a soldier was what a Massachusetts infantryman archly called "Horizontal Refreshments." A frequent order of business for a soldier lucky enough to draw a day's pass was a stop at a saloon, followed by a visit to one of the army of prostitutes who thronged the cities near the war zones and at times clustered about the camps. The same Massachusetts infantryman wrote buoyantly to a friend of the "gay old time" he had enjoyed in Washington drinking lager beer by day and "riding a Dutch gal" at night.

By 1862, Washington had 450 bordellos, which sported names like the Haystack, Hooker's Headquarters, the Ironclad and Madam Russell's Bake Oven. By one report, the city had at least 7,500 full-time prostitutes. For Federal soldiers with more liberal leaves, the red-light districts of New York

Flanked by family and servant, Colonel James McMahon of the 164th New York (center) plays chess with his regimental surgeon. During the tranquil months between campaigns, the wives and children of officers often lived at camp.

and Boston were the places to go, while men of the Western armies thronged to Cincinnati and Chicago. Alexandria, Virginia, across the Potomac from Washington, had so many bawdy houses that a wide-eyed Indiana infantryman reported it was "a perfect Sodom."

For the Confederates, Richmond was the center of prostitution. Women brazenly solicited on the grounds of the Capitol itself, and at one well-known brothel across the street from a military hospital, prostitutes exposed themselves in the windows, luring over so many recovering casualties that the hospital's superintendent lodged a complaint with the city.

In the field, a few enterprising prostitutes followed the armies, doing business out of their own tents or huts, or sometimes within the confines of the camps themselves. In October 1864 two prostitutes named Mary and Mollie Bell were caught in Confederate uniforms posing as one Tom Parker and Bob Morgan. They had been working within the ranks for nearly two years. The women were tried, found guilty and imprisoned for "aiding in the demoralization of General Early's veterans."

Venereal disease was not only prevalent but largely uncontrolled. About 8 per cent of the soldiers in the Union Army were treated for venereal disease during the War, and a great many cases went unreported. Figures for the Confederate Army, though sketchier, suggest the extent of the problem: In a single month in Richmond, the 10th Alabama alone reported 68 cases of venereal disease.

Treating it was a combination of guesswork and hope. The doctors experimented with such remedies as pokeweed, elderberries, mercury, zinc sulfate, silver nitrate and even cauterization. One Confederate surgeon prescribed "silkweed root put in whiskey," along with pills of resin from pine trees, and small pieces of blue vitriol. This potion, he contended, would "cure severe cases of ghonorrhea." In fact, his nostrums were useless, but a few others did alleviate the symptoms.

Less hazardous was the passion for gambling that swept camps both North and South. It was the universal time killer, deplored and sometimes banned by local commanders but perennially popular nonetheless. "Chuck-a-luck and Faro banks are running night and day, with eager and excited crowds standing around with their hands full of money," wrote a Mississippi soldier in 1862.

Dice and card games were the favorites, but soldiers would risk their money on anything: races, cockfights, boxing matches, baseball games or raffles. Men quartered near streams could be found fitting small boats with paper sails and racing them for wagers. And there was no letup in the gambling, even on Sabbath days. The colonel of the 7th Wisconsin noted that his regiment's

favorite diversion, the dice game chuck-a-luck, invariably outdrew the chaplain's services. "I think this unfair," he added dryly, "as the church runs only once a week but the game goes on daily."

Gambling surged with particular passion immediately after payday. The paymaster's arrival was "the panacea for all ills," wrote an Illinois infantryman, but frequently the money was lost almost before it was pocketed. "Down in the mouth," noted Jacob E. Hyneman of Grant's army in his diary. "Only paid a week ago and have not a cent now, having bluffed away all that I did not send home. I don't think I will play poker any more."

Some men gambled for the fun of it and some to augment their scanty funds as they

Private Billy Crump, orderly to Colonel Rutherford B. Hayes of the 23rd Ohio, returns from a foraging expedition in West Virginia laden with poultry, eggs and butter. Soldiers hungry for fresh food held a resourceful forager in high esteem. Hayes, who became President in 1877, appointed Crump as his White House steward.

awaited their pay. General John B. Floyd complained in 1862 that half of the men in his 51st Virginia Infantry had not been paid in six months: "They have not a single dollar to purchase the least little comfort, even for the sick." Later in the War, some Confederates would go a year and more without being given any money. Even in the wealthier North, some regiments would wait long periods for their pay: At one point, the 1st Massachusetts Cavalry, for example, went unpaid for nine months.

For officers, the situation could be grave; expected to purchase their own meals, they were in desperate straits if the paymaster was late and the commissary refused them credit. Captain De Forest recalled a day when he was reduced to eating nothing but a slice of watermelon. He was tempted to beg some hardtack from the enlisted men of his company, but decided against imposing on his soldiers. De Forest concluded that the irregular payment of salaries was "a fruitful source of demoralization" for the entire Army.

Indeed, the lack of money provoked not only foraging but outright theft and plunder. Since men of both the Union and Confederate Armies were often encouraged — if not compelled — to live off the land, it was not always easy to distinguish between theft and legitimate foraging. But certain units quickly acquired unsavory reputations for pillaging. One notorious regiment was the 6th New York, whose recruits were characterized by an officer as the "creme de la creme of Bowery society." It was rumored that a volunteer had to have a prison record before the 6th New York would accept him into their ranks. The regiment's own colonel had his gold watch lifted as he min-

gled with the men shortly before their departure for the front.

The Confederates, who fought mostly on home ground, tried harder to curb pillaging. Many Southern troops preferred to beg handouts from their people rather than take food by force. Yet hunger threatened to get the better of courtesy. A northern Virginia planter described in his diary the march of Lee's forces through his town in the summer of 1862: "The neighborhood is swarming with soldiers and the scanty stock of provisions is being rapidly devoured. The soldiers are considerate as under the circumstances would be expected, but they are starving and will be fed as long as there is anything left for them to eat."

Elsewhere, more desperate soldiers abandoned all notions of civility. A Confederate in Mississippi wrote: "I now have some idea of the devastating effects of an army marching through a Country. Our Soldiers act outrageously. They have not left a fat hog, chicken, Turkey, goose, duck, or eggs or onions behind." A Georgia infantryman watching the pillagers at work concluded that "I had almost as leave have the Yanks around my house as our own men."

Some foragers became legends for their exploits. Billy Crump of the 23rd Ohio, who served as orderly to Colonel Rutherford B. Hayes, future 19th President, once borrowed the colonel's horse and came back laden with 50 chickens, two turkeys, one goose, more than 20 dozen eggs and upwards of 30 pounds of butter. Another who won renown for his skills was the chaplain of a Union regiment in Louisiana. "Colonel," he would say, "the health of this battalion requires sweet potatoes, and I should like permission to take up a contribution."

The two types of punishment shown here were used to discipline Federal soldiers who had committed infractions such as insubordination, drunkenness or theft. One man, with his head shaved and wearing a sign detailing his crime, is drummed out of camp. Four others are paraded about in wooden barrels. These ritual humiliations were prescribed not by Army regulations but by long military tradition.

As foraging increased in the occupied South, there were occasional reprisals by the local people. Foragers who straggled behind their units might be found murdered and mutilated by the roadside — victims of some farmer's rage. A soldier in Sherman's army was discovered hanging from a tree with a note pinned to his body that read, "Death to all foragers."

Maintaining discipline was one of the most difficult tasks for the unseasoned officers of both Armies. The volunteer's independent nature and his generally low opinion of his superiors made him at times intractable. It was not uncommon for soldiers to curse their officers. "You are a God-damned, white-livered, tallow-faced skunk," an Irishman of the 30th Massachusetts shouted at his superior after receiving a harsh reprimand, "and if you say that again I will knock every tooth down your throat!"

Verbal assaults were sometimes overlooked, but it was impossible to ignore a physical attack on an officer. Offenders were either imprisoned or drummed out of the service with dishonorable discharges. The traditional ceremony for such discharges called for the guilty party to have his head shaved and his buttons and insignia torn from his uniform before the entire regiment. He was then marched between the silent, somber ranks of his former comrades and out of camp.

Punishment for lesser offenses was usually dependent on the whim of commanding officers. Some of those in charge were lenient, while others, in the words of John Billings, "felt that every violation of camp rules should be visited with the infliction of bodily pain." Thus there was a great deal of inequity in sentencing — and, consequently, much resentment among the troops. Hundreds of men, for example, were given no more than a little extra guard duty for overstaying their leaves. Yet one unfortunate and dull-witted Federal infantryman was given three years at hard labor for coming back to camp five days late. While some men caught stealing in camp were paraded about the company streets, others were hung by their thumbs.

The most common punishment for such slight offenses as insubordination or drunkenness was a few days in confinement. This might be in a guardhouse or stockade, a barn, a tent, an open pen, or simply a field marked off and patrolled by sentries. A prisoner could be there for as little as a few hours or as long as a month. In any case, it was hardly a terrible sentence, for it provided a welcome rest from regular camp duties. Perhaps sensing that this was more reward than punishment, Colonel Roger W. Hanson of the Confederate 2nd Kentucky made a practice of visiting his guardhouse every day to deliver lectures reminding prisoners of their transgressions.

Another common penalty was known as bucking and gagging. Gagged with a stick tied in his mouth, the offender was seated on the ground, his hands tied together in front of him. Then his knees were thrust up between his elbows, and another stick or pole was forced between arms and knees, pinning him in a dreadfully uncomfortable position. Seated thus for several hours in the sun, thirsty, cramped, and treated to a chorus of derisive howls from his campmates, a soldier had plenty of time to reflect on his crime — or, more likely, to nurture hate for the man who sentenced him.

Sometimes, punishment was tailored to fit the crime. A Union cavalryman who stole a saddle was forced to parade around camp for several hours with the saddle on his back. When a trigger-happy Confederate soldier shot a stray dog, his officers ordered him to carry the dead animal in his arms around camp at double-time. Another Confederate, caught selling whiskey, was mounted on a rail and carried through the camp with three bottles dangling on strings from his feet, and a sign around his neck reading "Ten Cents a Glass."

A fairly common punishment was the one given to a soldier from Texas who broke the rule against firing his rifle in camp. He was sentenced to carry a heavy log on his shoulder for three hours. "The first hour he done well," wrote a messmate. "The second hour he was walking slow and looking serious and changing the stick from right to left and from left to right and calling for the time of day, and long before the third hour was out he was begging for mercy."

Most men preferred to obey the rules and avoid the resultant penalties. And many soldiers eschewed the seamier side of camp life in favor of simpler pleasures. Among those who were literate, a great deal of read-

In a camp near Charleston, South Carolina, a fiddle-toting Confederate and his comrades relax outside a tent grandly dubbed "Music Hall."

An 1863 playbill touts a burlesque about Pocahontas, performed in Petersburg, Virginia, by members of a Confederate artillery battalion from New Orleans. So popular were their productions that playgoers came from Richmond, 20 miles away.

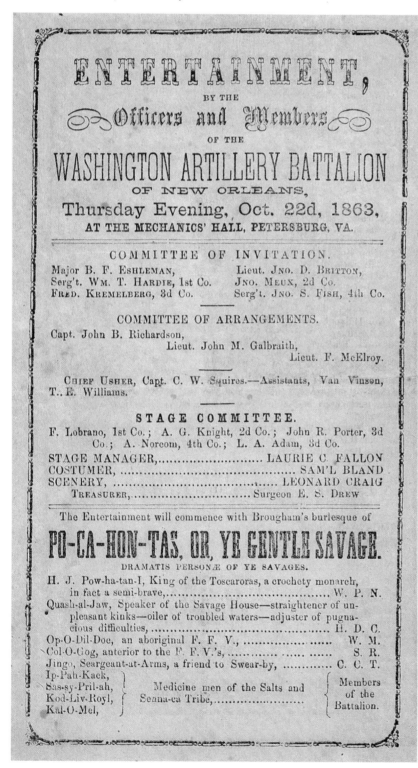

ENTERTAINMENT,

BY THE

Officers and Members

OF THE

WASHINGTON ARTILLERY BATTALION

OF NEW ORLEANS,

Thursday Evening, Oct. 22d, 1863,

AT THE MECHANICS' HALL, PETERSBURG, VA.

COMMITTEE OF INVITATION.

Major B. F. Eshleman,   Lieut. Jno. D. Britton,
Serg't. Wm. T. Hardie, 1st Co. Jno. Meux, 2d Co.
Fred. Kremelberg, 3d Co.   Serg't. Jno. S. Fish, 4th Co.

COMMITTEE OF ARRANGEMENTS.

Capt. John B. Richardson,
        Lieut. John M. Galbraith,
                           Lieut. F. McElroy.

Chief Usher, Capt. C. W. Squires.—Assistants, Van Vinson, T. E. Williams.

STAGE COMMITTEE.

F. Lobrano, 1st Co.; A. G. Knight, 2d Co.; John R. Porter, 3d Co.; A. Norcom, 4th Co.; L. A. Adam, 3d Co.

STAGE MANAGER,........................ LAURIE C. FALLON
COSTUMER, ... SAM'L BLAND
SCENERY, ... LEONARD CRAIG
Treasurer,.............................. Surgeon E. S. Drew

The Entertainment will commence with Brougham's burlesque of

PO-CA-HON-TAS, OR, YE GENTLE SAVAGE.

DRAMATIS PERSONÆ OF YE SAVAGES.

H. J. Pow-ha-tan-I, King of the Toscaroras, a crochety monarch,
    in fact a semi-brave,............................. W. P. N.
Quash-al-Jaw, Speaker of the Savage House—straightener of un-
    pleasant kinks—oiler of troubled waters—adjuster of pugna-
    cious difficulties,................................. H. D. C.
Op-O-Dil-Doc, an aboriginal F. F. V.,................. W. M.
Col-O-Gog, anterior to the F. F. V.'s,................. S. R.
Jingo, Seargeant-at-Arms, a friend to Swear-by, ... C. C. T.
Ip-Pah-Kack,   ⎫
Sas-sy-Pril-ah,   ⎪ Medicine men of the Salts and   ⎱ Members
Kod-Liv-Royl,   ⎬ Senna-ca Tribe,...................... ⎰ of the
Kal-O-Mel,   ⎭   Battalion.

ing was done. The Bible was most popular, followed by novels and newspapers. Well-funded regiments like the 13th Massachusetts had their own libraries. Poorer Confederate regiments like the 9th Kentucky were forced to forage for books. On the shelves of most camp libraries could be found the works of European authors such as Hugo and Scott, along with a sampling of Shakespeare and perhaps a few Greek or Latin texts. An orderly of the 9th Kentucky apologized to his colonel for bringing in a book in good physical condition but with what he called "damned bad print." It was a volume of Cicero in Latin.

The troops enjoyed such popular periodicals as the New York *Illustrated News, Frank Leslie's Illustrated Newspaper, Harper's Weekly* and the *Southern Illustrated News.* The *Waverly Magazine* was in demand for its personal ads placed by young women seeking "a soldier correspondent." Dime novels sold well in camp, and so did picture books offering "spirited and spicy scenes." In addition, scores of regiments produced their own newspapers. For two years, General John Hunt Morgan's renowned Confederate cavalry brigade printed the *Vidette,* whose satire aimed to mock the Yankees and entertain the troops.

Around campfires at night, the armies sang. If there was a good fiddler in the group — generally the case in predominantly rural regiments — the men might go through round after round of "Arkansas Traveler," "The Goose Hangs High" or "Billy in the Low Grounds." If there was someone with a concertina, jew's-harp, banjo or guitar, they might join in on "Oh Lord, Gals, One Friday" or "Hell Broke Loose in Georgia."

More popular still were sentimental bal-

lads — "When This Cruel War Is Over," "Just Before the Battle, Mother," "My Old Kentucky Home." The Civil War armies were not only sentimental but deeply impressionable. When spirits were at their lowest in the Army of the Potomac in the winter of 1862-1863, bands were forbidden to play the most popular of all Civil War songs, "Home Sweet Home," for fear of the devastating effect it would have on the morale of the homesick troops.

Some songs had a partisan appeal. Among the Federals, wrote Colonel Thomas Wentworth Higginson, who commanded a black regiment, "the John Brown song was always a favorite, at all times and seasons." Provided new lyrics by Julia Ward Howe in November 1861, it became "The Battle Hymn of the Republic." But Yankee soldiers preferred to march to their own versions of "John Brown's Body," which sprouted

fresh stanzas almost every month. North and South shared certain hymns — "Rock of Ages," "Amazing Grace" — but the Confederates claimed exclusive rights to such songs as "The Yellow Rose of Texas," "The Bonnie Blue Flag" and, of course, "Dixie."

In the larger, more permanent camps, the men often joined together to provide themselves with more formal activities and entertainment. A number of camps had Masonic Lodges. Others formed literary and debating societies and amateur theatrical groups. The 50th New York Engineers built their own timber playhouse at Petersburg, Virginia, in 1864, and in the winter of 1862-1863 at Manchester, Tennessee, the Confederate 9th Kentucky staged a farce entitled *Bombasties Furioso*.

In the winter, snowball fights were common occurrences in the camps. Often they began with two or three participants and es-

Off-duty Federal soldiers play a casual game of baseball. Enthusiasm among the troops helped to win national popularity for the sport. When they lacked proper bats and balls, soldiers improvised, slamming yarn-wrapped walnuts with rough staves, for example.

Spectators gather to watch a pair of Federal soldiers square off in a boxing match at a winter camp. Men often placed wagers on such contests.

Federal General Orlando B. Willcox and his staff look on as servants prepare to release fighting cocks in camp near Petersburg, Virginia, in 1864.

calated into virtual military exercises involving whole brigades. The 2nd and 12th New Hampshire engaged each other so vigorously one winter, observed a participant, that "tents were wrecked, bones broken, eyes blacked, and teeth knocked out." In a Confederate winter camp at Dalton, Georgia, in the late snows of March 1864, what began as an impromptu skirmish turned into a full-scale conflict, with the generals themselves entering the fray.

In warmer weather, there were individual and team sports. The men boxed, jumped, wrestled, ran races, hurdled and even bowled with cannonballs. But the most popular sport was the relatively new game of baseball, which then had rules so favoring the runner that the score soared. Once in 1864 the 13th Massachusetts beat the 104th New York 62 to 20.

In camps of both sides, no diversion occupied as much time as letter and journal writing. "Everybody is writing who can raise a pencil or a sheet of paper," noted a Virginian in July of 1861. The soldiers wrote out of love and homesickness and a desire to keep in touch with the world they had left behind. But there was another reason: the need to reflect on the strange, taxing and dangerous adventure they had embarked upon. At their best, the soldiers' letters and journals were full of acute observation and simple but vivid language. "You will smell hell here," a Louisiana Confeder-

ate warned a recruit bound for camp. According to a Federal infantryman, an unpopular officer did not know "enough to learn a dog to bark." A soldier from Ohio observed that Confederate dwellings near Fredericksburg looked "like the latter end of original sin and hard times." From Chattanooga, Private Michael Dresbach wrote his wife that he was so hungry he "could eat a rider off his horse and snap at the stirrups."

Some of the writing had an almost scientific tone. "I have been struck with the intensity of the mind's action and its increased suggestiveness after one has received a wound," wrote Oliver Wendell Holmes Jr. after being shot in the chest in his first battle, at Ball's Bluff. Exposed to enemy fire for the first time at Georgia Landing, Louisiana, Captain De Forest noted with wonder that "the terror of battle is not an abiding impression, but comes and goes like throbs of pain."

And running through the more reflective letters was a note of self-examination — a probing of one's own resources of courage and commitment. When he went off to war, Major James Austin Connolly of the 123rd Illinois Infantry expressed hope that his legs would not prove to be "of the 'Peace' persuasion," inclined to "rapidly carry me away from the first shot of a hostile gun." If his legs did not betray him, he added, he would trust himself to "the God of battles" and defend to the end his "government and its policy whether right or wrong."

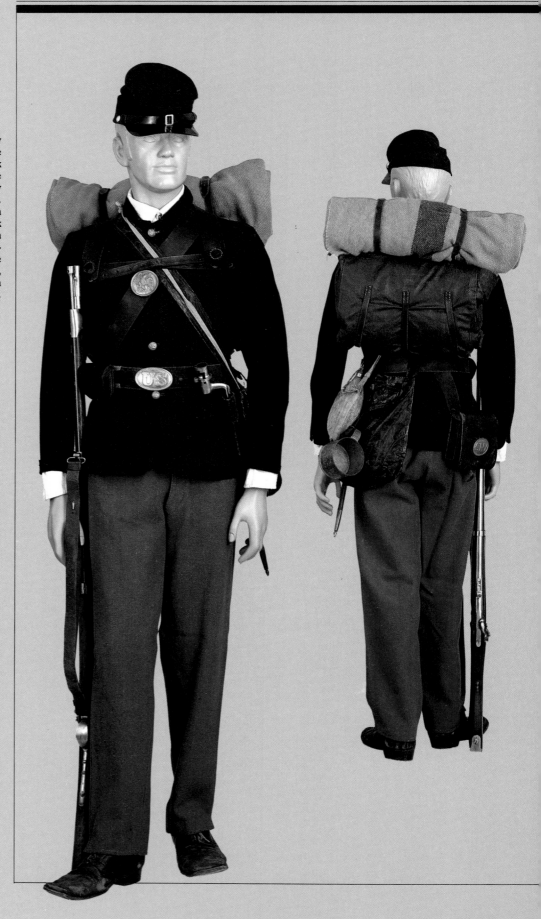

The Federal infantryman generally went to war garbed in a blue forage cap with black leather visor; a dark blue, loose flannel sack coat; blue woolen or kersey trousers; and blocky leather brogans called gunboats. Atop his knapsack he often carried a rolled wool blanket; inside the pack were his half of a two-man tent, a groundsheet, an overcoat and personal effects. A rifle, 40-round cartridge box, sheathed bayonet, cap box, haversack, cloth-covered tin canteen and tin cup completed the outfit.

Outfitting the Rank and File

The Civil War soldier carried on his back nearly everything he would need to fight the enemy and survive the elements. Because of shortages of cloth, dye and leather in the Confederacy, however, Federal troops were generally better equipped than their foes.

The assorted gear of a fully equipped infantryman — shown here and on the following pages — might weigh as much as 50 pounds. To lighten their load, soldiers on campaign often discarded what they viewed as excess items, particularly overcoats and other articles of clothing. One Federal general declared that an "army half the size of ours could be supplied with what we waste."

At the very least, the pared-down veteran had to tote a rifle with bayonet, a cartridge box, a haversack, blankets and a canteen, all held in place by canvas or leather straps crisscrossing the torso. This burdensome arrangement led one private to complain, "I can appreciate the feeling of an animal in harness now."

The typical Confederate soldier wore a slouch hat; gray or butternut wool shell jacket; gray, butternut or blue trousers; and low-heeled brogans. Slung across one shoulder and tied at the hip was his blanket roll, made up of a blanket and perhaps a groundsheet or a shelter-half wrapped around any extra articles of clothing. Other basic gear included a rifle, leather cartridge box with tin compartments, bayonet with scabbard, cap box, cotton haversack and heavy wood canteen.

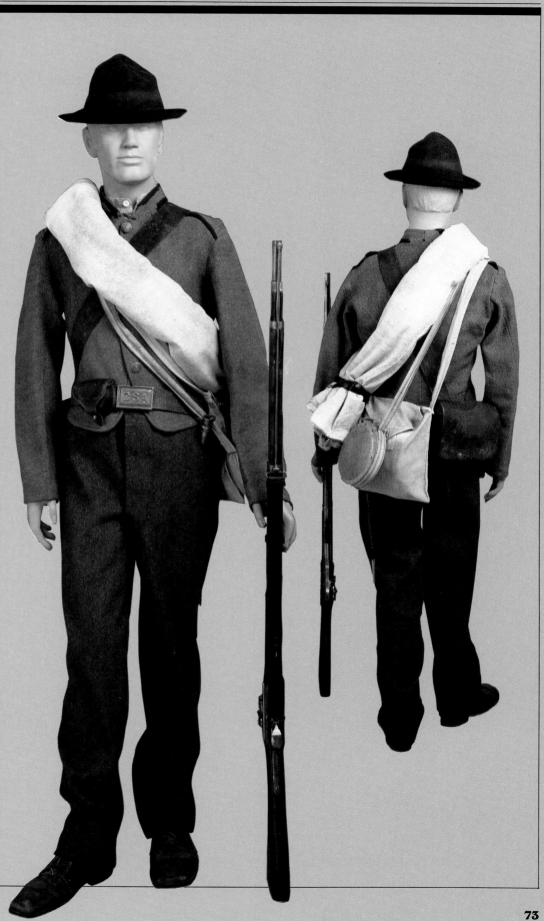

The Federal soldier's accouterments ranged from the essential — eating utensils, cup and sewing kit — to the extraneous, represented here by such items as the pipe, and the small lyre-shaped jew's-harp at lower right. Rations were carried in a haversack, with a removable pocket for perishables. Among other handy articles were a hinged matchsafe *(below)* and a spiked candle holder *(bottom row).*

The typical Confederate accessories, carried in a soldier's haversack *(right)* or in his pockets, are shown here; clockwise from top right, they are a razor, towel, soap, comb, jackknife, writing kit and mess kit, Bible, family portraits, change purse and bank notes, handkerchief, sewing kit, tobacco pouch, matches and pipe. The haversack was draped over one shoulder and rode on the opposite hip.

The Federal infantryman's extra clothing and protective gear included (*clockwise*) a blue caped overcoat of kersey, a gray wool blanket weighing five pounds, a gum blanket that doubled as tent floor and poncho, a heavy white flannel pull-over shirt, a shelter-half and a pair of wool socks.

The Confederate infantryman's drab wool overcoat with cape *(right)* was in short supply; most men did without or wore captured Federal coats. Other garments and gear included a homemade coverlet, a homespun cotton shirt, an oilcloth groundsheet, a homespun vest and wool socks.

The Wasted Legions

"Our wounded are doing badly; gangrene in its worst form has broken out among them. Those whom we thought were almost well are now suffering severely. A wound which a few days ago was not the size of a silver dime is now eight or ten inches in diameter."

NURSE KATE CUMMING WITH THE ARMY OF TENNESSEE, LATE IN 1863

"Future years will never know the seething hell and black infernal background," wrote the poet and journalist Walt Whitman of the Civil War, "and it is best they should not." Whitman was referring to the battle that was waged behind the lines — the grim struggle of the sick and wounded to survive. Too old to enlist, he spent much of the War nursing the diseased and the wounded as they fought the dread enemies of infection and fever. He was on hand to observe the rising tide of Federal victims returning from the front. He was witness to the desperate efforts to create facilities that could care for the huge numbers of ailing men. "It seemed sometimes as if the whole interest of the land, North and South, was one vast central hospital," he wrote, "and all the rest of the affair but flanges."

His impression was borne out by grim statistics. In the four years of conflict, more than 60,000 men died of wounds received in battle; perhaps six times that number died of disease. It was the enemy's shot and shell the soldiers feared, but they would come under fire only infrequently. Meanwhile, every day of their army life, they were in mortal peril from an invisible enemy — the microbes that flourished in the filth of their camps and on the very hands of their doctors.

Yet the appalling toll of sickness was hardly a failure of the military. The medical knowledge and resources then available to the authorities were paltry. Most of the older doctors had learned their craft by apprenticeship. Younger physicians, who would constitute the majority of Civil War doctors, usually had degrees of some kind, but those credentials could be deceiving. The medical schools of the time required nothing more for admission than that the applicant be of minimum age and able to pay the tuition, and the schooling itself took only two years.

Prewar medical treatment concentrated primarily on regulating the bowels, the kidneys and the blood. Enormous doses of all manner of medicines were administered to achieve a proper consistency of bodily fluids and excretions. A favorite drug was calomel, a compound of mercury used as a cathartic and administered so lavishly that mercury poisoning was a common aftereffect. The principal painkillers were opiates — usually laudanum or the more potent morphine. In an address to the Massachusetts Medical Society in 1860, the eminent practitioner Dr. Oliver Wendell Holmes heaped scorn both on the public, who in its love of patent medicines "insists on being poisoned," and on the medical profession's excessive prescribing of drugs: "If the whole *materia medica*, as now used, could sink to the bottom of the sea, it would be all the better for mankind, and all the worse for the fishes."

European doctors, especially in France, had made great strides in understanding the manner in which diseases spread and the benefits of surgically removing diseased tissue. Unfortunately, the new knowledge was slow to circulate and even slower to win acceptance. By 1860 a few American physi-

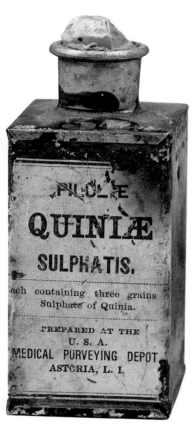

Tinned iron containers of quinine, a drug widely used in the treatment of malaria during the War, were part of the standard medical kit carried by Federal Army surgeons. To supplement the output of private pharmaceutical companies, the U.S. government set up manufacturing plants in Philadelphia and New York; altogether, some two million ounces of quinine were produced in the North.

cians had performed audacious and successful operations, but the scalpel was an unfamiliar tool to most doctors. And those who did perform surgery knew nothing about sterilization, or the ease with which infection could be introduced into an incision or wound. In fact, infection was expected, and festering — laudable pus, as it was called — was considered part of the healing process.

As the War began, the Federal Army had a total of 98 medical officers, the Confederacy 24. Many of these were veterans of long tours of duty at distant posts and were even further behind the medical times than civilian doctors. The director of the U.S. Army Medical Department deemed the purchase of medical books an extravagance; as for equipment, his agency owned just 20 thermometers and perhaps a half dozen stethoscopes.

In the early months of the War, volunteer doctors joined the ranks of both the U.S. and Confederate Medical Corps. Boards of examination were established to weed out incompetents, but many surgeons unfit for service — appointed through favoritism by state Governors or regimental colonels — slipped through. In time, both corps named medical inspectors to oversee their operations. That measure, combined with other reforms and practical experience in the field, helped to improve the care given the sick and wounded. By and large, however, the medical staffs would remain undermanned, underqualified and underequipped. Yet in 48 months of war, they would be called on to treat almost 10 million cases of illness and injury.

The first medical crisis appeared even as mobilization began; in their haste, Army recruiters failed to guard against the enlistment of diseased and unfit men. There were detailed regulations for the medical examination of recruits, but these rules were blithely ignored. Often the required physical examination at enlistment amounted to little more than confirmation that the recruit possessed the proper number of extremities. When Leander Stillwell joined the 61st Illinois, he was examined by what he called "a fat, jolly old doctor." The physician joked, stood him up, felt his shoulders, back and limbs, and gave him "two or three little sort of 'love taps' on the chest." That done, the doctor beamed and said to Stillwell's captain, "I only wish you had a hundred such fine boys as this one! He's all right, and good for the service."

Military officials took the attitude that any man fit to be a farmer or clerk was fit for soldiering. The 5th Massachusetts received cursory inspections from examiners who were without any medical qualifications, and soldiers in the 27th Indiana never saw a doctor at all until their first battle. Not only did an inestimable number of sickly and disabled men get into the Armies in the early stages of the War, but perhaps as many as 400 women posing as men bluffed their way through perfunctory medical examinations and enlisted. By late 1862, some 200,000 recruits originally accepted for service had been judged physically unfit and discharged, among them boys in their early teens and men over 60.

Even then, thousands of the infirm remained. Hospital beds needed for battle casualties began to fill with syphilitics, epileptics and elderly men with hernias — none of whom should have been admitted to the Army in the first place. As the War progressed and the shortage of manpower grew more acute, doctors became even more lax in their examinations. In Georgia in December of 1863, instructions issued by the state adjutant general limited the grounds for rejection of a recruit. The guidelines directed doctors to "exercise a sound and firm discretion and not yield your judgment in favor of every complaint of trivial disability." Besides, the adjutant general ventured, most infirmities were "strengthened and improved by the exposures incident to the life of the soldier."

The Georgia rules made it lawful to enlist recruits with any of a wide range of disabilities: a slight deformity, a speech impediment, heart problems, muscular rheumatism, myopia, hemorrhoids, a missing eye or absent fingers, a hernia, dyspepsia, a mild case of tuberculosis, or difficulty urinating. In all such instances, the examining surgeon was instructed to find the man fit for duty.

Even able-bodied recruits fell victim in droves to the maladies that awaited them in the Army. The men came mostly from farms and small rural communities; rarely had they congregated in large groups in confined spaces. Relatively few had been exposed to common communicable diseases — measles, chickenpox, mumps or whooping cough. As a result, when they arrived by the thousands at their first encampments, they were easy prey for viruses to which many of their city-bred companions were immune.

Measles was the worst. Surgeon L. J. Wilson of the 42nd Mississippi remembered the outbreak that occurred in his camp in 1861 as "something that astonished everyone, even the surgeons." Within three months, 204 men in three regiments died, and the doctors could do nothing. Wilson's 100-odd patients were crammed into an old tobacco warehouse, a space that measured only 60 by 100 feet. "The poor boys were lying on the hard floor," he wrote, "with only one or two blankets under them, not even straw, and any-thing they could find for a pillow. Many sick and vomiting, many already showing unmistakable signs of blood poisoning."

Contagious diseases hit just as hard among the Federals. Peter Wilson of the 14th Iowa wrote his wife in 1862 that "measles went through our Regiment in such a manner that out of 560 men, only 250 are on duty."

Various other ailments afflicted the men. Colds resulting from exposure to the elements often quickly worsened into bronchitis or pneumonia. The strange and often poorly prepared diet of salt beef or pork, hardtack and coffee prompted digestive ills. Within a few weeks, many a new regiment was seriously diminished. The 12th Connecticut marched to war 1,000 strong; it entered its first battle with just 600. The 128th New York, having seen only a smattering of action during its first year, could muster a mere 350 at the end of that period.

Gradually, as the men became accustomed to their circumstances and their systems became more inured to affliction, the incidence of common infectious diseases declined. But at the same time, the troops became increasingly susceptible to far more serious diseases spawned in the filth of the camps.

The Regular Army, out of long experience, had fashioned a lengthy set of regulations for maintaining the health of the men in the field. These required strict cleanliness in living quarters and food-preparation areas; personal bathing and regular airing of tents and bedding; careful placement and use of latrines and garbage pits, with daily applications of earth and chloride of lime; and protection of the purity of water supplies. But the volunteer units generally had no such experience, and if their officers did not understand or like the rules, they ignored them.

Documenting the Ravages of Battle

VIRGINIA PRIVATE, WITH GANGRENOUS WOUND

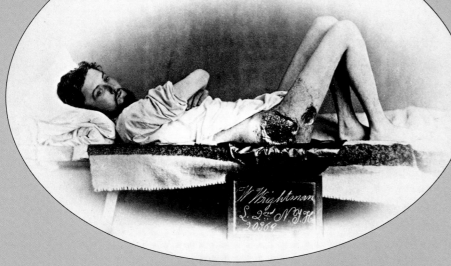

At the start of the Civil War, there was a dearth of reliable scientific information concerning the treatment of battle wounds. It was not long, however, before medical authorities for the Federal government realized that the unparalleled bloodshed — for all its horror — presented them with an extraordinary opportunity to fill that gap in the body of medical knowledge.

In 1862, Surgeon General Joseph K. Barnes ordered the 735 surgeons serving the Federal armies to file regular reports on every wounded patient in their care. Recognizing the value of photography as a recording tool, he directed the surgeons to have pictures taken of all "extraordinary injuries." He also asked them to send in "pathological surgical specimens" from their operations, including such items as damaged viscera, diseased joints and excised portions of bones.

Gruesome as the assignment may have been, surgeons in the field complied enthusiastically, and civilian doctors who took over the care of discharged veterans cooperated by sending along follow-up reports. The soldiers, for their part, willingly exposed their dreadful wounds to the camera in the hope that the record of their misfortune might someday prove valuable to medical science.

The surgeon general's study included evidence from the highest ranks: the leg of Major General Daniel Sickles, amputated at Gettysburg; a report on Brigadier General Joshua Chamberlain, shot through the pelvis; a photograph of Major Henry Barnum posing with a linen cord passing through his body from front to back along the route of a wound suffered at Malvern Hill; even an account of President Abraham Lincoln's fatal head wound.

Most reports, however, concerned injuries to common soldiers such as Private W. Wrightman of the 2nd New York Heavy Artillery (*lower left*), shot through the hip; or a Confederate prisoner, Private John L. Gray (*upper left*) of the 12th Virginia, shot in the foot and captured near Petersburg.

By the end of the War, some 318,000 Federal soldiers had fallen on the field of battle. But the valuable information gained from many of their case histories, as well as those of captured Confederates, contributed immeasurably to advances in the treatment of battle wounds.

NEW YORK ARTILLERYMAN, WITH HIP WOUND

Moreover, officers who depended for their positions on the votes of their subordinates tended not to be enthusiastic disciplinarians.

Thus it took years for some regiments to grasp the fact that sickness might be reduced — and the potability of their water greatly enhanced — if they stopped locating their trench latrines upstream of camp. To many men it simply did not matter where the stinking ditches were put: They would not use them anyway. They objected to the odor and the flies, and they were embarrassed to be seen in an open field in an undignified position. Instead, they simply relieved themselves behind the nearest bush or tent. Camp garbage, including the offal of cattle, was often left to rot wherever it happened to fall.

An inspector in late 1861 found most Federal camps "littered with refuse, food and other rubbish, sometimes in an offensive state of decomposition; slops deposited in pits within the camp limits or thrown out broadcast; heaps of manure and offal close to the camp." In 1863 a Virginia soldier confided to his diary that "on rolling up my bed this morning I found I had been lying in — I won't say what — something though that didn't smell like milk and peaches."

It is not surprising, then, that flies, lice and fleas swarmed all over the camps. "I get vexed at them and commence killing them," one Confederate said of the flies, "but as I believe 40 of them comes to every one's funeral, I have given it up as a bad job." Some

A company of the 10th Maine Volunteers is portrayed enjoying a bountiful Thanksgiving dinner at a camp near Annapolis, Maryland, in 1861. Such images were intended to reassure the folks back home that their boys were well fed and cared for. In truth, feasts like this one were rare.

soldiers joked that they found in their clothing lice with the letters *I.W.* engraved on their backs — evidence that the vermin were "In for the War." Even in battle the men were conscious of their passengers. In one fight, a Yankee colonel was seen waving his sword with one hand while feverishly scratching himself with the other. Such was the pestilence that someone adapted a common prayer to the situation: "Now I lay me down to sleep, / While graybacks o'er my body creep; / If I should die before I wake, / I pray the Lord their jaws to break."

Although most men were revolted by the filth and the vermin, neither the troops nor their doctors understood the real peril — the bacteria and viruses carried to the soldier by the insects. Thus carelessness compounded by ignorance led to devastating epidemics of dysentery and typhoid fever.

Bowel disorders constituted the soldier's most common complaint. There was much confusion between diarrhea, which is a symptom, and dysentery, a disease in its own right. The affliction of loose bowels was so widespread that it generated a soldier's lexicon; the men called it "the runs," "Virginia Quickstep," or "Tennessee Trots." A much-quoted proverb held that "bowels are of more consequence than brains."

George Maret of the 44th New York, himself afflicted, wrote that Army doctors took the malady for granted. At sick call, rather than performing an examination and arriving at a diagnosis, the surgeon simply asked him "What is the matter with you?" Upon being told, the doctor prescribed a dose of salts, which did nothing. The next day, the doctor prescribed more salts, and the day after, a couple of pills, followed by castor oil and laudanum. "That is sure to lay you flat,"

said Maret, and sure enough, the treatment made it impossible for him to eat, weakening him and making him more susceptible. Then it was off to the hospital to lie on the cold ground under a single blanket. "Sick dogs," he wrote, "are treated better than this."

In fact, not much could be done for the sufferers. Theories about the causes of the complaint abounded; they included defective diet, exposure, something called "crowd poison," overindulgence in coffee and breathing the effluvia of putrefying corpses. Just as the theories varied, so did the remedies tried — a host of patent medicines, herb and bark teas, diet regimens, and the wearing of a flannel "belly band" to prevent abdominal chills. None of these proved particularly successful. The Federal Army of the Potomac reported that in the first year of the War 640 out of every 1,000 men contracted diarrhea and dysentery; the next year the rate was 995 per thousand. According to one Confederate surgeon, "few soldiers ever had a natural or moulded evacuation."

A Southern minister wrote that chronic diarrhea seemed to break down the will power of the troops more than any other ailment of the War. "The patients seemed to lose not only desire to live but all manliness and self-respect," he wrote. "They whined and died in spite of all we could do."

Still, the death rate from dysentery remained low compared with the toll from typhoid fever. Perhaps one fourth of noncombat deaths in the Confederacy resulted from this disease, commonly called "camp fever." It was equally destructive in the Union. One Connecticut soldier told of 42 deaths in as many days in his regiment, with barely 225 left for duty, "and most of those staggering skeletons covered with fever sores." He

could only watch as the sick wandered in delirium, "jabbering and muttering insanities, till they lie down and die." Fortunately, in the last two years of the War, as sanitation improved and the immunity of the men increased, the incidence of typhoid declined.

Just as widespread, though less often fatal, was malaria. The "ague" or the "shakes," the soldiers called it, and their beliefs about its source, although expressed in terms of age-old superstitions, were not entirely without foundation. "Poisonous vapors" arising from stagnant water were blamed, and care was taken to camp upwind from swamps. The men did not, however, identify the real villain — the millions of mosquitoes bred in such waters and swarming in the air.

The use of quinine, a drug long known to reduce malaria's symptoms, helped to keep the number of fatalities low. Still, one of every four men who fell out at sick call suffered from the anopheles mosquito's bite. "We are more afraid of the ague than the enemy," wrote an Illinois soldier. In the 38th Iowa, 421 men out of 910 were either killed or incapacitated by the disease, and in the entire Federal Army, some one million cases of malaria would be reported during the War.

Although winter brought a respite from malaria, it aggravated other maladies. At Fredericksburg in the winter of 1862-1863, a man of the 13th New Hampshire wrote: "It is fearful to wake at night, and to hear the sounds made by the men about you. All night long the sounds go up of men coughing, breathing heavy and hoarse with half-choked throats, moaning and groaning with acute pain, a great deal of sickness and little help, near or in the future."

Such misery was reduced in those winter camps that were properly prepared and maintained, but winter campaigns could be deadly because of the weather alone. A soldier who marched with Stonewall Jackson into the Allegheny Mountains west of Winchester, Virginia, in January of 1862 reported that 11 men of the command froze to death at their posts. "Two of them, a little in advance of the others, were standing with their guns in their hands, as cold and as hard frozen as a monument of marble — standing sentinel with loaded guns in their frozen hands!" Seven months later, in a sweltering August heat wave, several members of the Stonewall Brigade would die of sunstroke on the march to the Battle of Cedar Mountain.

It hardly helped the soldier's well-being that his food was often as unsanitary and vermin-ridden as his surroundings. "We live so mean here the hard bread is all worms and the meat stinks like hell," complained one private, "and rice two or three times a week & worms as long as your finger. I liked rice once but god damn the stuff now."

In terms of bulk, the troops were reasonably well fed — at the outset of the War, at least. The mandated daily ration for a Federal soldier in 1861 included at least 20 ounces of fresh or salt beef, or 12 ounces of salt pork; more than a pound of flour; and a vegetable, usually beans. Coffee, salt, vinegar and sugar were provided as well. Confederate troops were allotted a similar ration.

Problems arose for both sides, however, when fast-moving armies outstripped their supplies. The Confederates suffered in addition from a lack of funds for the commissary departments and severe scarcities. Thus soldiers at times went hungry during the War. Near-starvation sapped the strength of the Union's Army of the Cumberland at Chattanooga in 1863 and sparked mutinies among the Texas Infantry and the Army of Tennessee. In the wake of Braxton Bragg's retreat from Kentucky, a Confederate officer watched his famished men gathering corn from the ground where horses had fed. Such pickings, he reported, were "for days the sole diet of all." In 1863 at Vicksburg troops under Confederate General John Pemberton implored him in a petition: "If you can't feed us, you had better surrender us."

Although most soldiers, most of the time, had enough to eat, complaints about the freshness and palatability of the food were often justified. Much sickness was caused by rancid beef. To counter this danger, beef was frequently pickled — infused with enough salt to preserve it for two years, as required by Army regulations. To be made edible, such "salt horse," as the men called it, had to be soaked in water so long that many nutrients were leached out along with the salt.

When in the field, soldiers saw little beef and few vegetables; they subsisted for the most part on salt pork, dried beans, hardtack or corn bread, and coffee. The men invariably prepared their meat — and often the bread and beans, after they were soaked — by frying it in great gobs of grease. The digestive ailments that resulted from this practice were innumerable, and one physician campaigned vigorously, but with little success, to spare his men "death from the frying pan" by persuading them to broil their meat.

Some of the beef issued to the Confederates proved so tough that a Louisiana officer threatened to requisition files so his men could hone their teeth for better chewing. When he later found shanks and necks in the beef sent to his camp, he pleaded with the commissary "for God's sake not to start throwing in the hoofs and horns." And North or South, fresh or preserved, the meat was soon infested with worms. One Yank reported sardonically that "yesterday morning was the first time we had to carry our meat, for the maggots always carried it till then. We had to have an extra guard to keep them from packing it clear off."

Hardtack, a staple in the Union Army, was probably the single most storied and despised article in the soldier's existence. Issued in the form of a cracker three inches square and up to half an inch thick, it was made of flour and water and was generally so hard as to be almost unbreakable, although it was by no means impervious to vermin. The crackers earned such sobriquets as "teeth-dullers," "sheet-iron crackers," and "worm castles." It was so difficult to eat the crackers in their native state that the men often soaked them in water, then fried the mess in grease to create a dish known as "hell-fired stew." In time, even the most fastidious no longer troubled themselves about the seething life inhabiting the cracker. "All the fresh meat we had come in the hard bread," a soldier wrote home, "and I, preferring my game cooked, used to toast my biscuits."

Confederates more often were issued corn bread. Made from coarse, unsifted meal, it was invariably overcooked and frequently wormy. The bread would get "so hard and moldy," complained a man of the Stonewall Brigade, "that when we broke it, it looked like it had cobwebs in it." When a soldier was issued raw corn meal, he generally mixed it with bacon grease and water and cooked it in his frying pan. The mixture, called "coosh," was at least filling, and many veterans preferred it to corn bread.

The vegetables were no better — when the

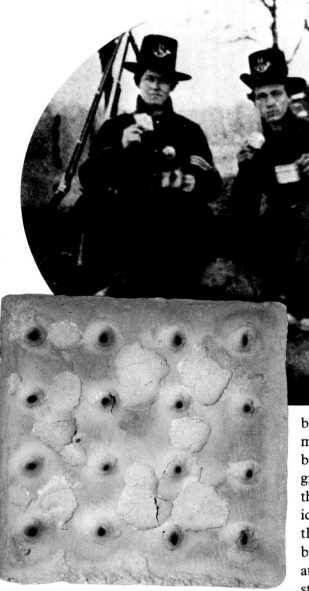

Three Federal soldiers enjoy a cup of coffee and a square of hardtack, the two staples of their diet. Hardtack, seen below at actual size, was a flour-and-water biscuit often infested with maggots and weevils after storage. Wrote one soldier: "It was no uncommon occurrence for a man to find the surface of his pot of coffee swimming with weevils, after breaking hardtack in it; but they were easily skimmed off and left no distinctive flavor."

men got them. There was scurvy in many camps from the want of the vitamins in fresh vegetables. Federal quartermasters tried to ease the deficiency by issuing "desiccated compressed mixed vegetables": hard cakes of dehydrated and pressed beans, turnips, carrots, beets, onions and more. The men called them "desecrated vegetables" or — after finding that the cakes also contained roots, leaves, vegetable tops and stalks — "baled hay." Confederate commissaries tried to make up for the lack of vegetables by advising the soldiers to eat wild onions.

The great indispensable of the soldier's diet was coffee. The brew was so firmly a part of American life that quartermasters la-bored hard to ensure that if only one commodity could be issued, it would be coffee beans. The men pounded the beans into grounds between rocks or crushed them with the butts of their rifles. Given five minutes' idle time, most soldiers would start boiling the grounds in water to produce a potent brew. While the shortage-plagued Confederates often had to make their brew with substitutes such as peanuts, potatoes, peas, corn and chicory, Federals enjoyed a ration of three or four pints of coffee a day. The men liked it dark and, as one F. Y. Hedley wrote, "strong enough to float an iron wedge." Provided it was served "innocent of lacteal adulteration," he said, "it gave strength to the weary and heavy laden, and courage to the despondent and sick at heart."

In fact, neither coffee nor the other staples of the soldier's diet did much to help maintain his health. Whatever the causes and contributing factors, the ravages of disease took an awesome toll. During the first year of the War, nearly 4,000 cases of sickness were reported for every 1,000 men in the Federal Army. This tide of illness placed an overwhelming burden on the undermanned and ill-prepared medical organizations. And it was but a prelude to the horrors to come, when the sick were joined by thousands upon thousands of battlefield casualties.

On the morning of Sunday, May 3, 1863, at Chancellorsville, the Union's Sergeant Rice C. Bull became one of the nearly half million Civil War soldiers who would fall wounded in battle. Like 94 per cent of the War's wounded, he was felled by a bullet (only 5.5 per cent were injured by artillery, the remainder by saber or bayonet). Statistically, his chances of survival were good — 7 to 1. But Sergeant Bull faced a terrible ordeal.

"I had just fired my gun and was lowering it from my shoulder," he wrote years afterward, "when I felt a sharp sting in my face as though I had been struck by something that caused no pain." Blood streaming down his face and neck, Bull calmly picked up his knapsack and headed for the rear.

Before each battle, it was the duty of the regimental surgeon to select a site for his field hospital. This was to be located beyond the range of enemy artillery, or about two miles to the rear. Usually the assistant surgeon also set up a forward aid station just outside the range of small-arms fire. While the surgeon prepared his instruments, the assistant surgeon organized the stretcher-bearers and orderlies, a complement of about 25 men made up of the hospital detail, the regimental bandsmen and any other available noncombatants such as the walking wounded. Later in the War, both sides organized corps of stretcher-bearers.

Sergeant Bull never made it to the facilities awaiting him. Partway there, he "felt another stinging pain, this time in my left side

just above the hip. Everything went black." When he regained consciousness some time later and found he could not get up, Bull called for help. The Federal lines were being overrun, and harassed stretcher-bearers took him a short distance to the rear and left him, along with scores of other wounded men, in a gully that afforded protection from the hail of fire in the still-raging battle. "No surgeon was with us and the men bringing back the wounded were too busy to give any aid," Bull remembered. "The wounded were very quiet as a rule and it was exceptional that they made loud cries or seemed excited."

Clear-minded but too weak to rise, Bull lay in his blood-soaked clothes. Like most men just wounded, he suffered a raging thirst; luckily he had a canteen and was able to drink from it while awaiting help.

Bull had been struck down by Minié balls, the most common Civil War small-arms ammunition. This conical bullet — .58-caliber and made of soft lead — distorted on impact to tear an enormous wound, generally carrying dirt, bits of clothing and germs into the violated tissue. The projectile was so heavy that it usually shattered any bone it encountered, and so slow-moving that it was likely to remain lodged in the wound.

Bull was luckier than some gunshot victims. Both the bullet that had entered his cheek and the one that struck above his hip had exited, leaving jagged holes in his neck and near his backbone, but missing bones and arteries. That he was wounded twice was not unusual. Many a soldier was hit several times in one battle. When a Confederate colonel struck down at Shiloh was asked where he was wounded, he replied, "My son, I am wounded in the arm, in the leg, in the head, in the body, and in another place

Within a shelter of cut foliage, officers and men of the ambulance detachment assigned to the Federal IX Corps gather for a photograph at their field headquarters near Petersburg, Virginia, in 1864.

which I have a delicacy in mentioning.''

Sergeant Bull, because his unit had been overrun, became a prisoner as well as a casualty. And the Confederate forces that won the day were unable to give food and proper medical care to their own men, let alone to the scores of Federal wounded. Bull and his comrades lay in the ravine from Sunday morning until Monday afternoon before the Confederates moved them to a central location — a field near an old log cabin — and another day passed before the worst cases were seen by Federal surgeons allowed to pass through the lines. This neglect was not prompted by animosity. Bull, whose wounds were not considered critical, reported that almost to a man the Confederates treated his fallen comrades kindly. This was, in fact, the policy of both medical departments.

Nonetheless, the failure to provide medical care to a wounded man within 48 hours — the length of time it took for most infections to set in — drastically diminished his chances of survival. And by that time, the anesthetizing effect of shock had worn off, escalating pain to agony.

Sergeant Bull endured all this and much more. For nine days he lay without medical attention among his sick and dying comrades, wracked with fever, in increasing filth, with little more to sustain him than an occasional sip of coffee. Even if food had been available, he would not have been able to eat it because of his cheek wound. At last, on May 12, he was paroled back to his army and put in a horse-drawn ambulance for a jolting, torturous 25-mile trip to a hospital at Aquia Creek. There, on May 13, his wounds at last were cleaned and dressed, and he was given nourishment, medication, a bath, fresh clothing and a bed. He not only survived his wounds, but reported back to his unit for active duty four months later.

Usually, every effort was made to treat wounded men within 48 hours. The policy was to get them as quickly as possible to the field hospital; attendants at the forward aid station limited themselves to stanching serious bleeding and providing a shot of whiskey, erroneously thought to counteract shock. Then the men were carried to whatever tent or shack was serving as the surgeon's headquarters and laid in ranks nearby, on blankets or straw pallets if they were lucky, on the bare ground if they were not.

The casualties were quickly divided into three categories: the mortally wounded, the slightly wounded, and those requiring surgery. Those about to die were made as comfortable as possible, then left alone. The men with minor wounds were attended to by a so-called dressing surgeon and given opiates or liquor. The surgical cases had to await their turn on the operating table.

Standing at a crude platform, often a door torn from its hinges, the hard-pressed surgeon performed his basic tasks: He did what he could to control any serious hemorrhaging; he probed the wound to locate and remove the bullet and any foreign objects; and, in many cases, he performed an amputation.

Before an amputation, a general anesthetic was usually administered. Despite the rumors of men being given only a chunk of wood or the proverbial bullet to clench between their teeth to prevent them from biting their tongues off during surgery, most received a liberal dose of chloroform. Remarkably few mishaps resulted from the lavish use of this chemical, which later came to be regarded as highly dangerous. Surgeons knew enough to periodically remove the

The Lifesaving Tools of a Surgeon's Field Kit

Using the instruments below, a surgeon could remove a mangled limb in 15 minutes. After anesthetizing the patient with ether or chloroform, he cut off the flow of blood to the wounded area with a tourniquet, cut away skin and tissue with scalpels and amputating knives, scraped the bone clean with a raspator and severed it with a surgical saw. Grasping the blood vessels with a tenaculum, he tied them off with silk thread, smoothed the stump with a gouging forceps and sutured the flaps closed.

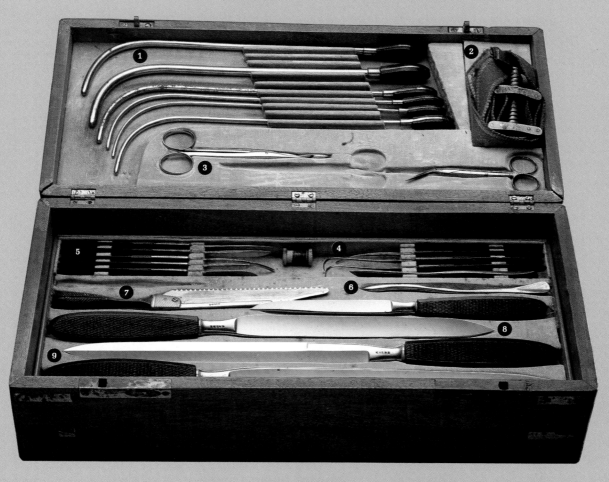

1. SOUNDS
2. TOURNIQUET
3. BONE FORCEPS
4. TENACULUM
5. SCALPELS
6. RASPATOR
7. METACARPAL SAW
8. AMPUTATING KNIVES
9. CATLINS
10. CONICAL TREPHINE
11. GOUGING FORCEPS
12. HEY'S SAW
13. TROCAR
14. DISSECTION FORCEPS
15. CAPITAL SAW

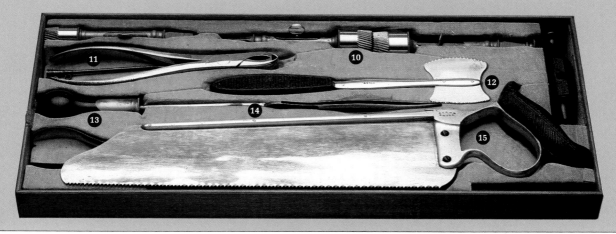

chloroform-soaked sponge or cloth held over the patient's nose and mouth, thus admitting what a Confederate doctor called a "free admixture of atmospheric air" — in plentiful supply in the open-air operating theater.

When the surgeon was simply probing a wound for a bullet, however, anesthesia was not considered necessary. Although specially designed metal probes were part of every physician's kit, surgeons preferred to use their fingertips in the interest of speed. If there was serious bleeding after removal of the bullet and any bits of cloth, dirt or bone in the wound, the surgeon often applied a ligature. As a means of stopping hemorrhaging, this procedure constituted one of the few innovations in surgical technique to emerge from the War. Yet it entailed a grave risk for the patient after surgery.

The method was simply to tie a loop of thread around the ruptured artery, leaving the end of the thread dangling from the wound or incision. Every day thereafter the doctor would tug at the thread until, the loop having rotted, the strand came away in his hand. If infection had reached the artery wall, however, or if a satisfactory clot had not formed, the premature tugging might open the artery and the patient might bleed to death on the spot. Indeed, this fate befell almost two thirds of the men so treated.

Three out of four battlefield operations performed during the War were amputations. This fearsome frequency provoked bitter criticisms, including repeated references to field surgeons as butchers. But as a surgeon in the Army of Tennessee, Derring Roberts, explained, "the shattering, splintering and splitting of a long bone by the impact of the Minié or Enfield ball were, in many instances, both remarkable and fright-

ful, and early experience taught surgeons that amputation was the only means of saving life." In fact, if the damaged tissue and bone were not excised, infection would soon set in and spread, dooming the patient.

The official policies of both medical departments regarding amputation were conservative; the surgeon was to save the limb if at all possible. But when a monstrously overworked field surgeon confronted a mangled arm or leg riddled with bone fragments, and realized that the victim faced a long, painful journey to a hospital, the case for amputation was often compelling. Of the 174,200 wounds of the extremities suffered by Federal troops, just under 30,000 led to amputation. Nearly three quarters of the amputees survived. Less complete figures for the Confederacy indicate similar proportions. However, when the amputation was delayed more than 48 hours, giving blood poisoning, bone infection or gangrene time to become established, the death rate doubled.

However justified, the surgeons' rush to amputate won them few friends in the ranks. Sergeant Bull complained that when Federal doctors reached him and his wounded comrades at Chancellorsville 48 hours after they fell, "the Surgeons began their bloody work at once in the immediate view of the wounded. As each amputation was completed the wounded man was carried to the old cabin and laid on the floor; the arm or leg was thrown on the ground near the table, only a few feet from the wounded who lay nearby." As cruel as the business was, the surgeons were doing whatever they could to save a few lives.

No soldier who witnessed field surgeons in action after a battle could forget the sight. After the First Battle of Bull Run, Adjutant

Attended by a nurse, Federal casualties of the battles at the Wilderness and Spotsylvania rest behind a temporary hospital in Fredericksburg, Virginia, on May 20, 1864.

William Blackford of the 1st Virginia Cavalry passed a clearing where the surgeons were hard at work. "Tables about breast high had been erected upon which screaming victims were having legs and arms cut off," he recalled. "The surgeons and their assistants, stripped to the waist and bespattered with blood, stood around, some holding the poor fellows while others, armed with long, bloody knives and saws, cut and sawed away with frightful rapidity, throwing the mangled limbs on a pile nearby as soon as removed." Other wounded awaited their turn, while more limped in or arrived on stretchers. The men who had survived their operations lay fanning the flies away from their bloody stumps. Blackford recalled that his men were soon overwhelmed by "the prayers, the curses, the screams, the blood, the flies, the sickening stench of this horrible little valley." All along his mounted column the men bent over their pommels, retching.

While most Civil War surgeons were aware that clean conditions somehow decreased the rate of infection, they did not know to sterilize their equipment. Sometimes water was so scarce that a surgeon went days without washing his hands or instruments. Instead, between cases he would wipe his bloody hands on a towel or his shirt and clean his knife with a swipe of his apron. Thus, as he finger-probed bullet holes or sawed at injured limbs, the surgeon was unwittingly the greatest agent of infection, passing microbes from one man to another.

The surgeons were scarcely indifferent to their patients' agony, and stress took a fearful toll on their own health. "We are almost worked to death," Surgeon George Stevens of the 77th New York wrote during the Wilderness Campaign in 1864. "My feet are ter-

Clara Barton was one of the first female nurses to seek out the Federal wounded on the battlefields, appearing with a wagonload of bandages, medicines and food. A surgeon who saw her at the front, stirring a huge kettle of soup, called her an "independent Sanitary Commission of one."

Louisa May Alcott, author of *Little Women*, served as a nurse at Union Hotel Hospital in Washington, D.C. The hospital conditions appalled her: "A more perfect pestilence box than this I never saw — cold, damp, dirty, full of vile odors from wounds, kitchens, and stables."

Dorothea Dix was appointed Superintendent of Female Nurses of the Federal Army in 1861. A rigid administrator, she was constantly at odds with doctors as well as her subordinates. She rejected thousands of nursing applicants for being too attractive, too young or "over-anxious."

Walt Whitman frequented the hospitals around Washington, D.C., dressing wounds and dispensing consolation and cheer. On September 8, 1863, he wrote his mother, "I believe no men ever loved each other as I and some of these poor wounded sick and dying men love each other."

ribly swollen; yet we cannot rest for there are so many poor fellows who are suffering." After the fighting started, Stevens worked four straight days and two full nights performing "those terrible operations."

"Oh! it is awful," he wrote. "It does not seem as though I could take a knife in my hand to-day, yet there are a hundred cases of amputation awaiting for me. Poor fellows come and beg almost on their knees for the first chance to have an arm taken off. It is a scene of horror such as I never saw. God forbid that I should see another." Yet in the following days, he saw one after another of the men die. "They look to me for help, and I have to turn away heartsick at my want of ability to relieve their sufferings."

Most who survived their wounds and the ministrations of the field hospital still faced a long period of recovery, and they were moved as soon as possible to the general hospitals — so named because they accepted patients regardless of regimental affiliation — that were established in many cities near the war zones. Early in the War such hospitals simply did not exist, nor were they contemplated; the head of the U.S. Army Medical Department denied a request to create a hospital in occupied coastal South Carolina because, he said, "the mild climate of South Carolina deletes the necessity of a hospital."

The wounded from the early battles were housed in converted schools, hotels, factories, railroad stations and private homes. But in a remarkably short period of time, both North and South had constructed a network of hospitals of astonishing size and commendable efficiency. By War's end, the Union Army was operating 204 general hospitals averaging more than 500 beds each. In the South, roughly 150 general hospitals

Chimborazo Hospital, sprawling on a hill near Richmond, was the Confederacy's chief medical complex. Its network of single-story pavilions served 76,000 patients during the course of the War. An esteemed administrator of the hospital was Phoebe Yates Pember (*inset*), a middle-aged widow from Richmond.

were built east of the Mississippi; 49 sprang up in Richmond alone, including Chimborazo Hospital, the largest in the Confederacy.

Chimborazo was a sprawling complex of 150 wards with a capacity for more than 8,000 patients. It had a bakery that could turn out 10,000 loaves of bread a day, a 400-keg brewery, five ice houses, a soap factory, cultivated fields and large herds of livestock.

For all their resources, the general hospitals were themselves breeding grounds of disease. Here the dreaded infections known as surgical fevers took hold, exacting an additional toll in human misery and death. Chief among them was blood poisoning. Over 97 per cent of those afflicted by it died. Another highly contagious infection, erysipelas, raged through the wards, achieving epidemic proportions but killing relatively few. And a chronic bone inflammation, osteomyelitis, plagued many patients, causing fever, pain and the exuding of pus for many years after they suffered a bone wound.

Perhaps the most awesome of the surgical fevers has never been diagnosed because it became extinct after the War was over, without revealing itself to modern medicine. This was the so-called hospital gangrene, which appeared as a small black spot on a wound or incision. Swiftly and implacably, the black area of dead and rotting tissue spread until it enveloped an entire arm or leg. Later in the War, surgeons learned through trial and error that excision of the dead tissue and applications of bromine effected a prompt cure.

In the main, however, the surgical fevers raged unchecked through hospitals of the North and South, claiming the weak patients, while doctors experimented with myriad medications. Gradually it was realized that several common hospital practices

A broadside intended for the families of war victims advertises the services of an embalmer in Philadelphia. Families who wanted their dead returned home for burial had to pay to have the corpse disinterred, embalmed and shipped back in a coffin.

EMBALMING THE DEAD.

PRESERVING
AND
PETRIFYING THE DEAD

The undersigned will attend in all the details to the preservation of the bodies of the DEAD entrusted to their charge, and every embalment will be conducted under the supervision of a skillful surgeon.

PERSONS AT A DISTANCE

Desiring to have the bodies of their deceased friends, on the field of battle or elsewhere, disinterred, embalmed, disinfected, or prepared and sent home, can have it PROMPTLY attended to by application to the undersigned, at the office of SIMON GARTLAND, 35 *South Thirteenth Street, Philadelphia.*

N. B.—The Process being the Original ROSSEAU Process, no Zinc, Arsenic or Alcohol is used.

PERFECT SATISFACTION GUARANTEED.

Respectfully refer to all the FACULTY *in every City where we are known.*

Doctors EATON & MACKAY,
CARE OF SIMON GARTLAND,
35 S. THIRTEENTH ST., PHILAD'A.

actually encouraged the diseases, and these were changed: Windows that had been shut at night to protect against supposedly noxious night airs were thrown open, and new hospitals were designed for maximum ventilation; the practice of reusing dressings, even those applied to horribly infected wounds, after a casual washing was discontinued; and increasing emphasis was put on cleanliness and the isolation of infected patients.

Slowly the quality of nursing in the hospitals improved as well. A wounded man might see a doctor once a day; any other human comfort came from his wardmates or the nursing staff. At first, nursing duties were assigned to convalescent or otherwise non-combatant soldiers who were usually ill-suited and always untrained for the job.

Although a few trained Catholic sisters served here and there early on, it was gen-

erally considered improper for women to work in hospitals. Despite the well-known achievements of Florence Nightingale in the Crimean War, cynics claimed that women would faint at the sight of blood and disturb the wounded with their hysterics. Sheer necessity soon made a mockery of such notions. For lack of anyone else to do the job, women were not only admitted to the wards, but actively recruited. The U.S. Congress provided for the use of female nurses in August of 1861; the Confederacy, typically slower to give way to such a departure from tradition, followed suit in September of 1862. A number of these women — Phoebe Y. Pember, Dorothea Dix, Clara Barton, Sally Tompkins and Louisa May Alcott among them — won national attention for their efforts.

Still, for all the strivings of the Armies to build more and better hospitals, and of the medical staffs to improve their care, confinement to a Civil War hospital remained a nightmare for many. Private Alexander Hunter of the 17th Virginia Infantry recalled the torment of his stay at a hospital in Petersburg, Virginia. At night, he wrote, his ward became "like the dim caverns of the catacombs, where, instead of the dead in their final rest, there were wasted figures burning with fever and raving from the agony of splintered bones, tossing restlessly from side to side, with every ill, it seemed, which human flesh was heir to. From the rafters the flickering oil lamp swung mournfully, casting a ghastly light upon the scene beneath."

Private Hunter emerged from the "dim caverns" a healed man. But legions died in such sad surroundings. By War's end, nearly a half million soldiers had perished of wounds or disease.

Soldiers' graves lie row upon row near a Federal hospital at City Point, Virginia. Many of the mounds were unmarked or designated simply by a stake bearing a number.

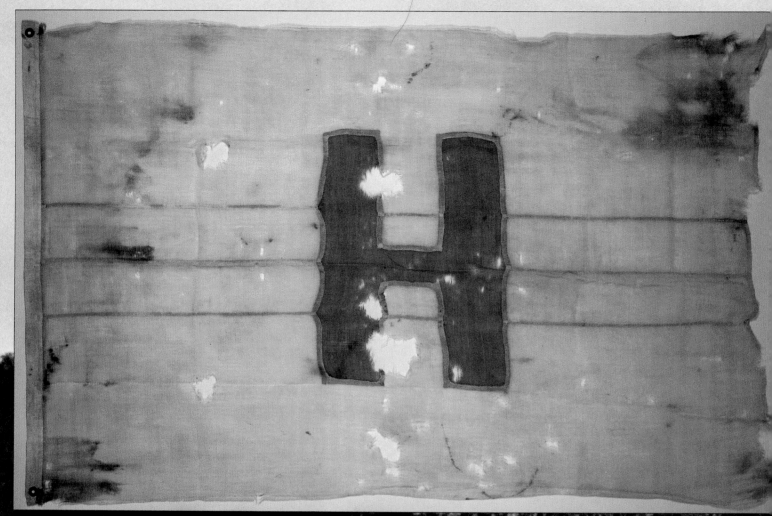

The Odyssey of the Wounded

Ambulances of the 57th New York Volunteers assemble in front of the regiment for a drill near Fredericksburg, Virginia, in 1864. The vehicles transported the wounded to field hospitals marked by yellow flags (*left*).

"I was wounded Saturday p.m.," Private Richard Ackerman of the 5th New York wrote his parents after taking a ball through the thigh in the Second Battle of Bull Run. "I laid on the battlefield for 48 hours and then rode in a government wagon for 48 hours more. Last night at one o'clock my wound was dressed for the first time."

Ackerman's ordeal was not unusual. When the War began, neither side had an efficient system for dealing with casualties. The first ambulances were bouncy two-wheeled carts known as "hop, step and jumps." Although these gradually gave way to more stable four-wheeled wagons, the jolting ride over rutted roads could mightily compound the agony of the wounded, and casualties would sometimes suffer contusions from the journey.

Rail and water transport to hospitals in the rear was usually comfortable by comparison. Yet wounded men were sometimes left stranded for days in railroad cars. On other occasions, casualties were packed tight aboard converted riverboats and coastal steamers that lacked even the most rudimentary medical equipment.

In spite of the enormous efforts made to improve hospital facilities during the War, many men who survived the trip to the rear later succumbed to their wounds. Private Ackerman wrote his parents, "Don't think it hard I had to be wounded, for I consider it a merciful dispensation of Providence I wasn't killed." But in late December 1862, four months after he wrote those words, Ackerman died of complications at a Federal hospital in Alexandria, Virginia.

Wounded soldiers recover from surgery on the grounds of a Federal field hospital near Fredericksburg, Virginia, in 1864.

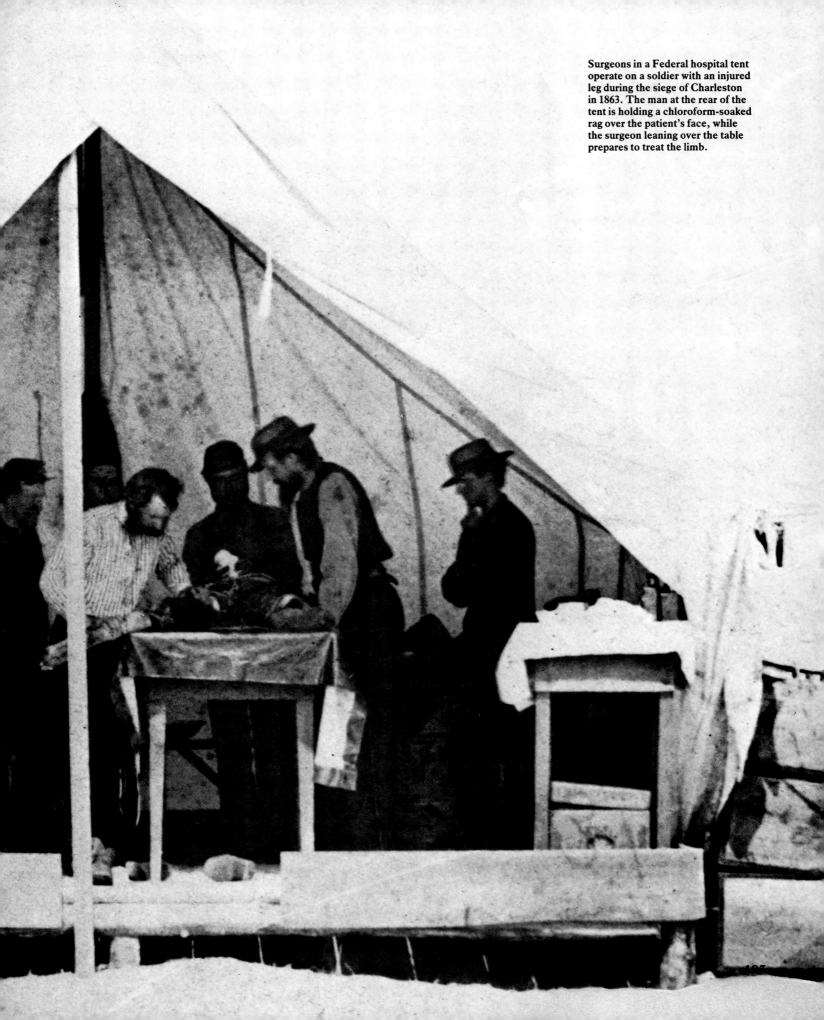

Surgeons in a Federal hospital tent operate on a soldier with an injured leg during the siege of Charleston in 1863. The man at the rear of the tent is holding a chloroform-soaked rag over the patient's face, while the surgeon leaning over the table prepares to treat the limb.

An ambulance convoy pauses in its journey to the large Federal hospital at City Point, Virginia, during the siege of Petersburg in 1864. Four-wheeled ambulances like these had folding bunks for wounded men. At times the vehicles were so grossly overcrowded that patients were in danger of being smothered en route.

Federal soldiers wound‐ during the siege of Vicksbu‐ crowd the decks of t‐ *Woodford*, a former Miss‐ sippi riverboat comma‐ deered to serve as a hospi‐ ship. The steamer evacuat‐ thousands of men to hos‐ tals in Baton Rouge and Ne‐ Orleans before it r‐ aground and sank in 186‐

Federal casualties of the Battle of Gaines's Mill await transport to the rear aboard flatcars near Richmond in 1862. A locomotive eventually arrived and hauled them to a field hospital at Savage's Station. Many of the men were later captured when the hospital was taken by the enemy.

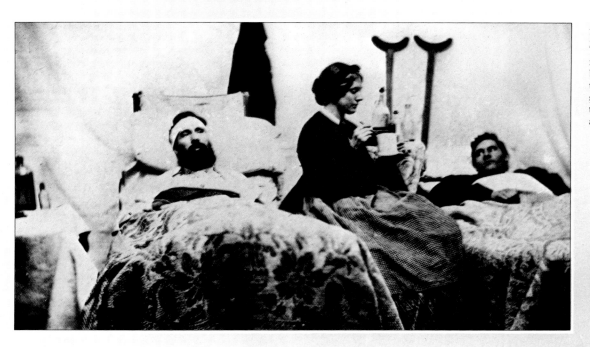

A nurse tends to two recuperating Federals at a hospital in Nashville, Tennessee. Hundreds of female nurses, most of whom were recruited by private relief agencies, served in the permanent hospitals of both sides. Though many lacked formal training, they helped bathe, bandage and comfort the wounded.

Patients lie abed under canopies of mosquito netting in a newly built wing of Harewood Hospital in Washington, D.C. The War spurred a massive construction program to cope with the large numbers of wounded. Such wards were usually one or two stories high and capable of accommodating 40 to 60 patients.

Rows of tents house the overflow of wounded on the grounds of Douglas Hospital in Washington, D.C. By late 1864, the Federal capital and environs had 25 large hospitals, and beds for more than 21,000 patients.

Soldiers at a Rhode Island convalescent hospital, some of them crippled for life, gather for a group portrait in 1864. The rehabilitation of disabled veterans fell mainly to private relief agencies, which organized recreational activities for the patients and tried to ease their return to civilian life.

Carriages bearing friends and relatives are drawn up before the visitors' entrance to Camp Convalescent in Alexandria, Virginia, the main center for Federal patients after their discharge from the area's hospitals. The pleasant setting was deceptive. As many as 15,000 men were quartered here under conditions so intolerable that the inmates called the place "Camp Misery."

The Prisoners' Plight

"When I was taken prisoner I weighed 165 pounds, and when I came out I weighed 96 pounds, and was considered stout compared with some I saw there."

PRIVATE A. S. CLYNE, 63RD NEW YORK, AN INMATE AT ANDERSONVILLE

On a winter day in 1865, a Confederate boat put in under a flag of truce at Cox's Landing on the James River, 10 miles downstream from Richmond, to deliver into Federal hands a cargo of prisoners of war. At the landing, a Federal detachment waited to transfer the paroled prisoners to a vessel that would take them back to their lines. "In a few moments," a soldier of the 13th New Hampshire recalled, "six hundred of our men were on the shore; they were hatless, shirtless, shoeless, wrapped up in old bed-quilts, their feet wound with rags, and many of them barefoot (and the wintry, ice-cold mud six inches deep). Their clothing was in tatters, their hair long and matted, dirty and unshaven, and all looked as pale and thin as though wasted with consumption or fever. Many were carried on board our boat on stretchers, too weak and sick to stand."

So debilitated were the ex-prisoners that it took two hours to transfer all of them to the Federal vessel. When the heavily laden craft finally pulled away from Cox's Landing, a military band struck up "The Star-Spangled Banner." The men raised a feeble cheer.

The scene was repeated, with variations, many times during the Civil War. The exchange of prisoners was always a grim reminder of the deplorable conditions prevailing in almost every wartime prison, North or South. No issue during the War stirred such violent passions or inspired such embittered accusations. Yet neither side started out with the intention of abusing prisoners of war.

The abuse that developed was the result of lack of resources — and lack of foresight.

Neither side expected to hold great numbers of prisoners. So unprepared were the Union and the Confederacy to deal with captured men that in 1861 there was no coherent policy for the handling of prisoners and not a single military prison on the continent capable of holding more than a handful of men. Even after the bombardment of Fort Sumter, neither side made immediate preparations for the care of prisoners; Southerners believed the War would be short, and Northerners expected to win it in 90 days. It was widely assumed that during this brief conflict, defeated parties would be granted the same terms of surrender accorded Major Robert Anderson and his entire Fort Sumter garrison, who were shown every courtesy and allowed to return to their comrades.

Yet such was the confusion surrounding prisoner policy that shortly after Major Anderson and his command marched unimpeded out of Fort Sumter, about 1,500 Federal troops in far-off Texas were being herded into makeshift detention camps. These men were United States Regulars who had surrendered to the Texas authorities after Texas seceded from the Union on February 1, 1861. At first promised safe passage out of Texas and the right to keep their arms and equipment, they were now being detained because of Confederate fears of the strength they would bring to the North. Most would spend the next two years in prison — the first

Confederate soldiers captured in Tennessee stand before a prison barracks at Camp Douglas in Illinois shortly after their incarceration in February 1862. They wear ill-fitting coats, provided by their captors, and prisoner-of-war identification tags.

the two sides on the question of prisoners.

Early in 1862, fighting resumed in earnest, and the increasing number of men captured posed a gigantic dilemma. Lincoln had by then acknowledged a state of war, but it was not until July of 1862 that the two governments agreed to set up a cooperative system of prisoner exchanges. Enlisted men were to be exchanged one for one, as were officers of equal rank. Beyond that, there was a complex scale of values: A major general was worth 30 enlisted men, a captain was worth six, a sergeant or a corporal was worth two, and so forth. Prisoners who could not be immediately exchanged were to be paroled — sent home under an agreement not to fight again until the other side received an equal number of parolees.

Implementing the agreement led to a mountain of paper work, and for this, too, the governments were unprepared. The system worked well for less than a year. Its inherent weakness was that it rested upon gentlemen's agreements, and the War quickly passed the boundary of gentlemanly conduct. Southern leaders refused to exchange black soldiers. Northern generals accused the Confederacy of violating the understanding concerning the use of paroled soldiers in battle. In May 1863, the agreement disintegrated, with each side charging bad faith. Of necessity, the number of prisons increased dramatically. Jails, training camps, warehouses, school buildings, even open fields were commandeered as holding pens.

By this time, each side had placed an official in charge of prisons: Lieutenant Colonel William Hoffman for the Federals and Brigadier General John H. Winder for the Confederates. Lieutenant Colonel Hoffman, named commissary general of the Union

men inducted into a vast army of Federal and Confederate prisoners whose history makes one of the saddest chapters of the War.

Fortunately for both sides, there was little action — and few prisoners taken — during the remainder of 1861. The only major battle in the East, at Bull Run, yielded about 1,300 Federal prisoners and just a dozen Confederates. In the West, the only significant action was at Wilson's Creek in Missouri, where the tally of prisoners taken by both sides barely exceeded 300. These were manageable numbers; most of the captives were held in a few tent camps, and neither side felt pushed to develop extensive prison systems. Moreover, individual commanders frequently acted on their own to arrange informal prisoner exchanges, even though President Lincoln's refusal to acknowledge a state of war or to recognize the legitimacy of the Confederate government precluded negotiations between

Guarded by the Federals seated in the foreground and those silhouetted against the tents at rear, Confederate troops captured in the Shenandoah Valley in 1864 line the slope of a Union camp, awaiting the journey to prison barracks.

Army, was an energetic, conscientious and highly motivated man, but he failed to grasp the magnitude of his task. Early in the War he was asked to establish the first Federal prison specifically designed for captured Confederates. An island seemed a logical site, preferably one well to the north. He looked over several islands in Lake Erie and rejected them on various grounds — too near to Canada, too expensive to rent, too close to a mainland saloon that might prove excessively attractive to the prison guards.

But his search of the lake finally turned up something suitable — Johnson's Island, two and a half miles offshore from Sandusky, Ohio. Figuring on a maximum of 1,000 prisoners, Hoffman pushed ahead vigorously and was able to announce the opening of the Johnson's Island prison in early 1862. Two weeks later, in Tennessee, Fort Donelson fell, and Hoffman had 15,000 prisoners on his hands; they were scattered about the North wherever shelter was available.

The Confederacy's General Winder had an even worse time of it. He too was unprepared for his task, and he possessed fewer material resources for coping with the flood of prisoners. Furthermore, while his mandate allowed him to oversee individual prisons, he lacked the authority to implement a uniform policy for the treatment of all prisoners in the South. In fact, no Confederate official had such authority. Winder did establish a few new camps, but most Federal prisoners were crammed into makeshift quarters, where they faced tribulations that rivaled the ordeals of combat.

For most men taken by the enemy, the dismal journey to captivity began in a temporary holding pen near the battlefield. After their names and units had been recorded, the prisoners of war were moved to the rear — on foot, or by boat or rail when transport was available. Frequently, civilians clustered along their route to gawk and sometimes to threaten. Private George Hegeman of the 52nd New York recalled traveling with other prisoners through Warrenton, Virginia, and attracting large numbers of "the Reb Ladies who before when our army passed through the town were all Union." Now, he added dryly, they "came out in their true colors and gave us a beautiful blessing, using the choicest language."

Eventually, the captured men arrived at their various detention centers, far from the front lines. All told, more than 150 places were used by the two sides as prisons during the War. The Federals tended to adapt public buildings to the purpose; the Confederates liked to use converted tobacco warehouses, which usually had good water supplies and could be transformed into prisons with comparatively little work.

On both sides, officers and enlisted men were sent to separate facilities. But no matter the rank of the inhabitants, conditions within the walls were abominable. "It is useless to attempt a description of the place," declared an Alabama officer incarcerated at Fort Delaware. "A respectable hog would have turned up his nose in disgust at it."

Much of the suffering of the prisoners was simply due to the pressures of war. In the South, prisoners were poorly housed and inadequately clothed largely because the necessary supplies were not available. The miserable rations that were handed out to Southern prisoners were often no worse than those Confederate soldiers were eating in the field. Indeed, the Confederate Congress passed an act early in the War specifying that "the rations furnished prisoners of war shall be the same in quantity and quality as those furnished to enlisted men in the army of the Confederacy."

The North was less often short of supplies, but reports of starvation in Southern prisons encouraged Federal officials to make prisoner rations a low priority. When a Confederate officer complained to Commissary General William Hoffman about the "inhuman treatment" he had suffered at Camp Chase near Columbus, Ohio, Hoffman replied that the treatment was "retaliation for innumerable outrages which have been committed on our people." Many people in the North believed that Rebel prisoners were being coddled. "How different an example of humanity the North is setting," wrote one newspaper correspondent, adding that captured Confederates were growing fat. The adjutant general of Ohio spoke of the "sleek fat rebels" lounging about Northern prison camps, and the Union's Quartermaster Gen-

Soldiers of the 11th New York Zouaves, captured at Bull Run on July 21, 1861, pose inside their prison, Castle Pinckney, in Charleston Harbor. The Zouaves, members of the New York City Fire Department, hand-lettered the signs in the background to poke fun at their plight.

eral, Montgomery C. Meigs, accused prison authorities of treating their inmates "as Southern gentlemen," and feeding them so richly that "they die of gout."

A study of conditions in both Northern and Southern prisons was undertaken by the United States Sanitary Commission in 1864. The commission's conclusion, summed up in a biased and inflammatory report, was that Confederate prison authorities had endorsed outrageously cruel practices and deprivations as part of "a predetermined plan for destroying and disabling the soldiers of their enemy." The report claimed that in Northern prisons, by contrast, Confederate soldiers had plenty to eat; mess funds had been provided so generously that there was even a surplus, which was being used to buy the prisoners luxuries. In response to such fanciful reports, Commissary General Hoffman made progressively heavier cuts in prisoner rations — thereby saving nearly two million dollars, which he proudly returned to the Federal Treasury late in the War.

Although a prisoner who had managed to hold on to his money after capture could supplement his diet with purchases from prison sutlers, few were so fortunate. The fact was that, North or South, the inmates were never far from starvation. A South Carolinian noted that his daily prison fare at Point Lookout, Maryland, was a half pint of "slop water" coffee for breakfast and a half pint of "greasy water" soup for dinner, followed by a small piece of meat. "The writer has known large, stout men to lay in their tents at night and cry like little babies from hunger," he said.

The meat and bacon available to men on both sides was described in letters and journals as "rusty" and "slimy" — and the other fare was no better. A Confederate declared that the soup at Fort Delaware came filled with "white worms, half an inch long." It was a standing joke, he wrote, "that the soup was too weak to drown the rice worms and pea bugs, which, however, came to their death by starvation." But to near-starving men, any fare would do: "Ate it raw," reads one entry in Private George Hegeman's diary, presumably referring to his meat ration. "Could not wait to cook it."

In the absence of adequate protein, prison rats were staple fare. "We traped for Rats and the Prisoners Eat Every one they Could get," wrote a soldier of the 4th Arkansas at Johnson's Island. "I taken a mess of Fried Rats. They was all right to a hungry man, was like Fried squirrels." And no matter what they ate, the prisoners learned to eat their food quickly for fear it might be seized by their messmates. Vicious and sometimes deadly brawls exploded over a few morsels of spoiled meat.

More often than not, drinking water in the prisons was tainted. One Confederate found Point Lookout's supply "so impregnated with some mineral as to offend every nose, and induce diarrhea in almost every alimentary canal. It colors every thing black in which it is allowed to rest, and a scum rises on the top of a vessel if it is left standing during the night, which reflects the prismatic colors as distinctly as the surface of a stagnant pool."

The barracks in many prisons were primitive structures — wet, cold and unsanitary. In a communication to William Hoffman, U.S. Secretary of War Edwin Stanton made it clear that in the North primitive housing should be the rule: "The Secretary of War is not disposed, in view of the treatment our prisoners of war are receiving, to erect fine establishments for their prisoners." In keeping with this injunction, the builder of the prison at Rock Island was told by Quartermaster General Meigs that the barracks "should be put up in the roughest and cheapest manner, mere shanties, with no fine work about them." At Camp Morton in Indianapolis, the barracks had no floors and were so flimsy that the snow and rain blew through them. Inmates at Libby Prison in Richmond complained that there were no panes of glass in the windows and that often there was no fire in the heat stoves.

At most installations, filth built up inside and outside the barracks, inviting swarms of pests. "The vermin was so plenty," observed a Rhode Islander, "that the boys said they had regimental drills." A Confederate at Old Capitol Prison in Washington, D.C., good-naturedly remarked how he and his mates would get together against the insects and have "a promiscuous slaughter, regardless of age or sex. But they must recruit from the other side, like the Yankee army, as we can notice no diminution in the forces." Noting the infestation of the Camp Douglas barracks in Chicago, the president of the U.S. Sanitary Commission remarked that "nothing but fire can cleanse them."

Infested garments could not be discarded, for there was little other clothing available. Many prisoners, particularly the Confederates, arrived in the camps with their uniforms in tatters. The need for clothing was so acute that the living seized the garments of those who died. Prisoners in much of the South experienced mild winters. But in the Federal camps, inmates had to endure ice and snow, and overcoats and blankets were scarce. At Johnson's Island, ill-clad Confed-

Commissary General William Hoffman, in charge of Confederate prisoners in the North, was infamously frugal. He told the commander of a prison camp in Indiana that "so long as a prisoner has clothing upon him, however much torn, you must issue nothing to him."

erate prisoners from the Gulf states suffered intensely from the winter winds off Lake Erie that cut through their barracks almost unimpeded. Survivors of the camp bore vivid memories of some of their comrades freezing to death on the bitter New Year's Day of 1864. Acknowledging the problem of deficient clothing, Hoffman gave some of the prisoners new Federal uniforms that had been rejected for field service.

Considering all that the prisoners suffered, the wonder was not that so many of them became sick, but that anybody at all managed to stay well. Confederate Surgeon Joseph Jones's description of what he found

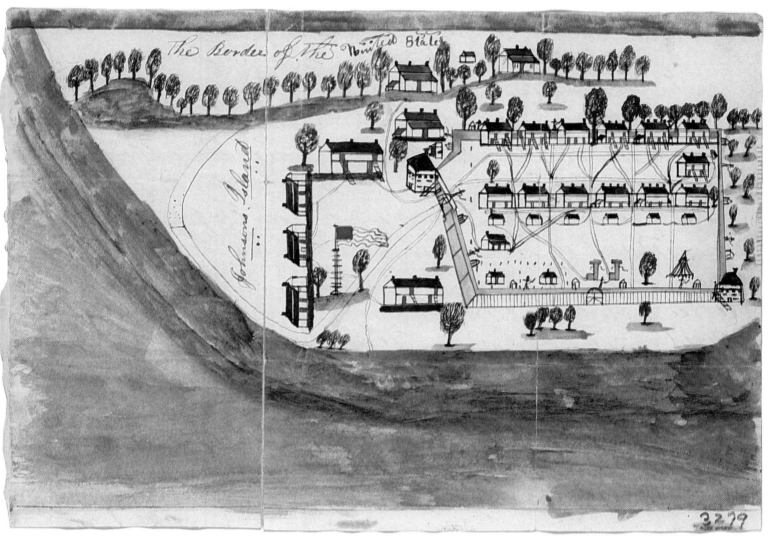

The Border of the United States

Johnsons Island

3279

This watercolor map of the Confederate officers' prison on Johnson's Island in Lake Erie was created by an inmate on the back of a letter home. Another officer, Major Henry Kyd Douglas, voiced his fellow prisoners' distaste for the Midwestern winter, noting that Johnson's Island was "just the place to convert visitors to the theological belief that Hell has torments of cold instead of heat."

at the infamous Andersonville camp in Georgia could have been applied to many other prison compounds. "From the crowded conditions, filthy habits, bad diet and dejected, depressed condition of the prisoners," Jones wrote, "their systems had become so disordered that the smallest abrasion of skin, from the rubbing of a shoe, or from the effects of the sun, the prick of a splinter or the scratching of a mosquito bite, in some cases took on a rapid and frightful ulceration and gangrene."

Survivors of the camps remembered how men used to press a thumb into their flesh to see if a discoloration was left in the indentation. That meant scurvy. Victims of the disease would lose their teeth, along with their hair. Then they could not walk. Finally they died. Sometimes scurvy reached epidemic proportions. Just three months after a prison camp opened in 1864 at Elmira, New York, 1,870 cases of scurvy were counted. At Fort Delaware between November 1863 and February 1864, at least 1 of every 8 Confederate prisoners suffered from the disease. Fresh vegetables could have cured the problem, and they were available for purchase at Fort Delaware. But Colonel Hoffman insisted that only absolute necessities be bought, and vegetables were considered a luxury. Thus $23,000 remained in the Fort Delaware relief fund, even as hundreds of men languished with scurvy.

Prison hospitals were feared almost more than the diseases they were supposed to treat. At Chicago's Camp Douglas, sick Rebels lay in the hospital on cots that did not have mattresses, sheets or any other sort of bedding. In January and February of 1863, men died there at the rate of six a day, while twice that number died in the barracks each day, unable to find space in the hospital. At Andersonville, where the hospital occupied five acres outside the main stockade, the patients lay on bare boards in sheds without walls. Naive hospital attendants, who frequently were paroled prisoners, cleaned wounds by pouring dirty water over them; the water then seeped into the earth, providing a breeding ground for insects. Flies swarmed over the patients, laying their eggs in open wounds.

Those who felt strong enough might organize their own activities or diversions to pass the time. Few books were available in the prisons, though, and even fewer newspapers. Some camps had copies of the Bible, and at uncertain intervals mail and packages came from home. Illinois Cavalryman John McElroy recalled that he became so starved for reading matter that he went through a copy of *Gray's Anatomy*.

Other prisoners played cards, checkers or chess, rolled dice or marbles, pitched ball or stones, or whittled trinkets from bone or wood. A few took daily walks over paths they had traced a thousand times before.

The prisoners' conversations tended to gravitate to the same tantalizing topic: the possibility of being exchanged or released outright, the chances of making it home. Prisoners were permitted to write letters, but these were heavily censored and usually limited to one page. A surprising number of men managed to keep intimate journals, using whatever scraps of paper they could find and employing ink made from rust.

Some found solace in religious services or in prayer. "Often while walking the floor of the prison, I repeat the Lord's Prayer," wrote a Confederate prisoner on Johnson's Island, "and I find my whole mind absorbed upon the subject of my future state of existence or my appearing before God." Although there was no official provision for services in the prison camps, the men sometimes held their own. At Camp Chase and at Johnson's Island, poker games were suspended while chaplains among the inmates preached sermons of hope.

Some of the prison commandants were deeply troubled by the sufferings of the inmates, and such officials were universally respected. At Johnson's Island, recalled one inmate, Colonel Charles W. Hill was regarded as a "good friend to the prisoners, all of whom esteemed him very highly for his kindness of heart." Much the same was said of Lieutenant Colonel Robert C. Smith, who commanded the Confederate prison at Danville, Virginia. Indeed, Smith was said to be such "a kind, sympathetic man" that the plight of his prisoners and his inability to improve it drove him at last to the bottle. Another commandant intimately concerned with his prisoners' welfare was Colonel Richard Owen at Camp Morton in Indianapolis. He was so respected by his former prisoners that after the War they commissioned and paid for a bust of the colonel, which was placed in the Indiana statehouse.

More frequently, however, Civil War prison officials were regarded by the men under their control as the embodiment of all the evils of the system. One inmate described Libby Prison's Richard Turner as "a vulgar, coarse brute," and "the greatest scoundrel that ever went unhung." Another recalled that Turner once kicked a dying man for no apparent reason. A prisoner at Fort Delaware averred that Lieutenant Abraham Wolf exhibited "all the mean, cowardly, and cruel instincts of the beast from which his name was taken." And one witness reported that Point Lookout's Major Allen Brady galloped his horse through crowds of prisoners, trampling those who were unable to step aside.

Although prisoners sometimes exaggerated the defects and deficiencies of their commandants, there seems no doubt that many of the officials were unfitted for their posts and owed them to political influence. One such commandant was Colonel Charles Allison, in charge at Camp Chase. A Federal inspector found Allison "entirely without experience and utterly ignorant of his duties," and noted that he was "surrounded by the same class of people." But, added the inspector dryly, "he is a lawyer and a son-in-law of the Lieutenant-Governor."

For the most part, the prison guards were equally incompetent. Their ranks were generally filled by inexperienced militiamen or — less often — by tired veterans. "We are under the Malishia," wrote an inmate at An-

dersonville of his guards, "& they are the Dambdst set of men I ever had the Luck to fall in with yet." Another prisoner thought the Andersonville guards "the worst looking scallawags," and remarked that they were either too young to hold a rifle or "old men who ought to have been dead years ago for the good of their country."

Prison inmates soon learned to distinguish between the behavior of the raw militiamen and the veterans. As Confederate Lieutenant McHenry Howard of the 1st Maryland Infantry recalled, it "was like the difference between bad and good weather." Imprisoned at Fort Delaware in the spring of 1864, Howard had ample opportunity to observe the demeanor of the 157th Ohio National Guard, a green regiment assigned to garrison duty at the camp. The militiamen's conduct toward the prisoners, he wrote, "was atrocious, devilish in the apparent desire to insult and practice small cruelties." They regularly confiscated personal possessions of the prisoners and opened fire on them at the slightest provocation.

On the other hand, when the Ohio Guard was replaced by the veteran 6th Massachusetts, Howard related, "the cursing and other abusive conduct immediately stopped: they behaved to us in a soldier-like and I may say gentlemanly manner and often spoke contemptuously of the actions of their predecessors."

Where veterans stood guard, there seemed to be a bond between fighting men that transcended sectional differences. In a few instances, prisoner and keeper even became close. Lieutenant Alonzo Cooper of the 12th New York Cavalry was guarded at Columbia, South Carolina, by a Confederate veteran who became such a "noble friend" that he

A Sampler of Prison Art

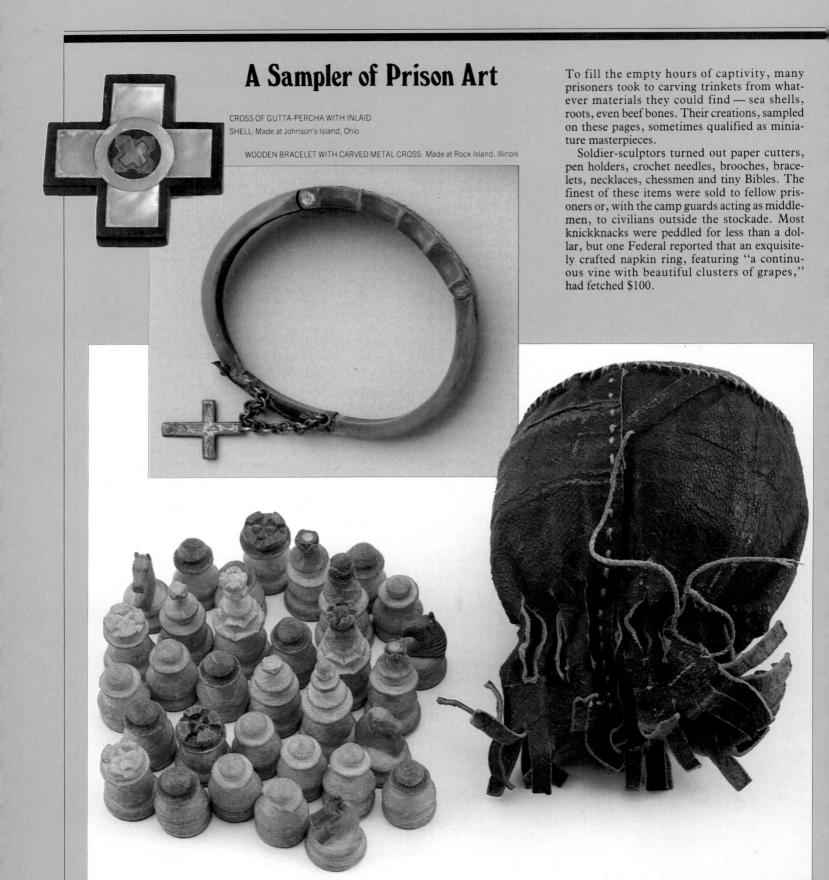

CROSS OF GUTTA-PERCHA WITH INLAID
SHELL: Made at Johnson's Island, Ohio

WOODEN BRACELET WITH CARVED METAL CROSS: Made at Rock Island, Illinois

To fill the empty hours of captivity, many prisoners took to carving trinkets from whatever materials they could find — sea shells, roots, even beef bones. Their creations, sampled on these pages, sometimes qualified as miniature masterpieces.

Soldier-sculptors turned out paper cutters, pen holders, crochet needles, brooches, bracelets, necklaces, chessmen and tiny Bibles. The finest of these items were sold to fellow prisoners or, with the camp guards acting as middlemen, to civilians outside the stockade. Most knickknacks were peddled for less than a dollar, but one Federal reported that an exquisitely crafted napkin ring, featuring "a continuous vine with beautiful clusters of grapes," had fetched $100.

WOODEN CHESS PIECES AND LEATHER POUCH: Carved by Captain Nathaniel Rollins, 2nd Wisconsin Volunteers, at Libby Prison, Richmond

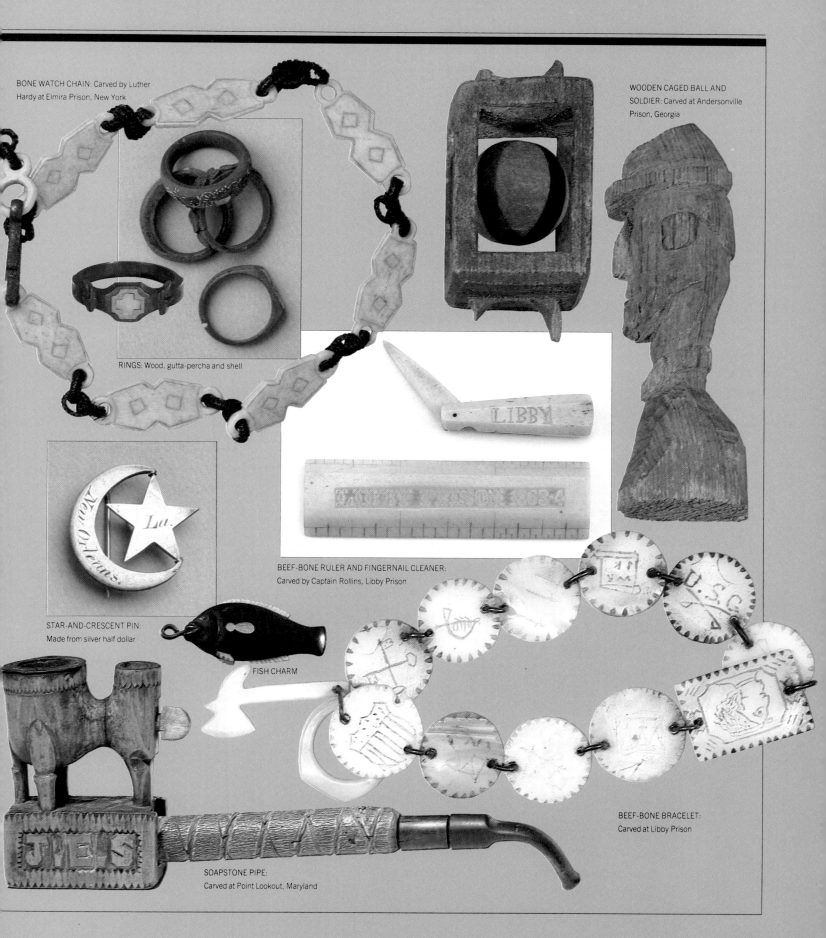

BONE WATCH CHAIN: Carved by Luther
Hardy at Elmira Prison, New York

RINGS: Wood, gutta-percha and shell

WOODEN CAGED BALL AND
SOLDIER: Carved at Andersonville
Prison, Georgia

LIBBY

BEEF-BONE RULER AND FINGERNAIL CLEANER:
Carved by Captain Rollins, Libby Prison

STAR-AND-CRESCENT PIN:
Made from silver half dollar

New Orleans

La.

FISH CHARM

BEEF-BONE BRACELET:
Carved at Libby Prison

SOAPSTONE PIPE:
Carved at Point Lookout, Maryland

looked the other way while Cooper and his comrades stole out of camp one night and broke for freedom.

Some prisoners received help from civilians, who risked being considered disloyal to express their sympathy for the captured men's plight. Colonel Harrison C. Hobart of the 21st Wisconsin Infantry recalled that while he and other prisoners were being held outside Atlanta after the Battle of Chickamauga, "kind-hearted people came out of the city, bringing bread with them, which they threw to us across the guard line." At a camp outside Charleston, Private Hegeman discovered that "the ladies here are kind and generous — the Irish women in particular. They come up and throw loaves of bread, tobacco, rice, etc." They continued to do so, he added, "notwithstanding the threats of the guard to bayonet them."

While prisoners found friends from without, they also faced enemies from within. There were violent regional conflicts, like the fight at a Richmond camp between New York and Kentucky prisoners. And there were constant personal disputes; in Richmond, for instance, one prisoner killed another for stealing his blanket.

More serious was the organized crime conducted by inmate gangs, which drew members from big-city slums in particular. An especially vicious gang calling itself the Moseby Raiders terrorized the Federal prisoners at Andersonville. Headed by William Collins of Pennsylvania, the Raiders robbed and murdered until they virtually dominated the camp. At last the other prisoners organized a resistance and, with the permission of the commandant, arrested and hanged six of the Raiders' ringleaders. Eighteen other members of the gang were forced to run the gantlet by their fellow prisoners, and three of them were beaten so severely that they died.

To escape from this nightmare world was the dream of every prisoner. As a Yankee at the Danville, Virginia, prison wrote, "Freedom was more desired than salvation, more sought after than righteousness." The guards assigned to escort men to prison were often lax, and many a man escaped back to his own lines while en route to confinement. Thousands more made the attempt from the compound — most without success.

In December 1864, one of the most ambitious escape plans of the War took shape in the prison warehouses of Danville. The captives were kept on the upper floors of the buildings, though every evening a few were allowed to come down to get supplies of water and firewood. One of the prisoners, Brigadier General Alfred N. Duffié — a French adventurer who had actually been relieved of his command shortly before his capture — plotted an elaborate scheme with Colonel William C. Raulston of the 24th New York Cavalry.

According to their plan, the two of them, acting as the evening water detail, would go downstairs and occupy their guards in conversation while the other men gathered at the stairwell on the floor above. Then Duffié and Raulston would overpower the guards, and the prisoners would rush down, pouring out of the building and into the neighboring warehouses. The escapees would capture the other guards, seize all the weapons they could, and free the entire prison population. That done, they would destroy Danville's military facilities and take off for friendly lines in the Shenandoah Valley.

Among the 8,000 Confederate officers held at Fort Delaware (*below*), on Pea Patch Island in the Delaware River, was Presbyterian minister Isaac Handy, shown at right leading a prayer service. An inmate recalled that the minister "labored like an apostle, and his influence went far to counteract the evil tendencies of prolonged prison life."

The plan went awry almost from the start. The two sentries were overpowered, but a sergeant outside looked in and called the alarm. Immediately the warehouse door was barred on the outside. "Too late, go back!" Duffié yelled to his men, who had charged down from above. Back up the narrow stairs they scrambled. Raulston was among the last. As he passed an open window, a guard outside fired through it. Raulston fell, wounded in the stomach. "Boys, I guess my goose is cooked," he said. Raulston was taken to a hospital, where he died. No one ever again attempted to escape from Danville.

But the urge for freedom waxed strong elsewhere, and occasionally it was rewarded. Confederate Brigadier General John Hunt Morgan and several of his Kentucky cavalrymen managed to tunnel their way out of the Ohio State Penitentiary at Columbus and escape. And a mass breakout — far and away the largest of the War — occurred at Richmond's Libby Prison on February 9, 1864.

This prison, which confined Federal officers only, was one of the most notorious of all Rebel compounds, densely crowded, teeming with vermin, and incurably drafty. It sat just a few blocks from downtown Richmond, with the James River only a hundred yards or so away. Its four floors contained 1,200 or more officers at a time. They were rarely allowed outside. "We fumed and fretted," wrote one inmate, "and our restraint grew more and more irksome. At last we settled down to the conviction that we were in for the war, unless we effected escape."

Thirty-one-year-old Colonel Thomas E. Rose of the 77th Pennsylvania was not about to wait for the War's end to regain his freedom. Captured at Chickamauga in September of 1863, he began thinking of escape almost as soon as he reached Libby Prison. With a Federal cavalryman from Kentucky, Major Andrew G. Hamilton, Rose tried several times to dig his way out, without success. Yet he persisted. From the barred upper-floor windows, Rose could see a 50-foot-long open field on the east side of the building. A tall board fence marked the field's far end, with a shed on the other side. If he could dig a tunnel from the prison to the shed, he could emerge without being detected by the guards.

In the center room on the main floor was an abandoned kitchen that was open to the prisoners. By cutting out a hole in the back of its fireplace, Rose could gain access to an unused basement below. A man could crawl through the hole, drop 10 feet and work undetected in the dark room underneath. Here Rose began his tunnel, enlisting a number of others in his enterprise, and swearing everyone to secrecy.

The men dug in shifts, sometimes around the clock when the guards were not bothersome. They had only primitive tools: knives, an old chisel, a wooden box until recently used as a spittoon, some string and a few candles. The excavation was excruciatingly difficult. Colonel Harrison Hobart wrote that "two persons could work at the same time. One would enter the hole with his tools and a small tallow candle, dragging the spittoon after him attached to a string. The other would fan air into the passage with his hat, and with another string would draw out the novel dirt cart when loaded, concealing its contents beneath the straw and rubbish of the cellar."

Through January of 1864 the work went on. By the officers' own calculations, the tunnel was about eight feet below street lev-

Brigadier General Alfred Duffié helped plot the abortive breakout of Federal officers from the Danville prison. Duffié, a former French Army cavalry lieutenant, had won four medals for bravery in the Crimean War.

Colonel William C. Raulston of the 24th New York Cavalry was shot at close range by a guard when the Danville prison breakout was discovered. He died five days later, the lone casualty of the incident.

el, and it was just big enough for a man to claw his way through by groping with hands and feet.

Then on February 7, 1864, one of the prisoners, Colonel Abel D. Streight, stepped forward. In the spring of 1863 he had led a bold but unsuccessful raid through Alabama with infantrymen mounted on mules, surrendering in the end to General Nathan B. Forrest. Now Streight declared that the tunnel was long enough. As the senior officer involved, he insisted on being the first to crawl through the tunnel and break free. It would look good on his record, and perhaps atone in some measure for his failure as a raider.

Fortunately Streight made his attempt at night, for when he stood up and poked his head out of the hole into the open air, he found that he was still several feet short of

the board fence, and perilously close to two sentinels standing in the open field.

Streight overheard one of the guards say: "I have been hearing a strange noise in the ground there."

"Nothing but rats," replied the other, and the two of them walked away.

Barely daring to breathe, Streight crawled back to report the near miss. Using a shirt to plug the hole in the ground, the prisoners resumed their digging with renewed vigor — painfully aware that if some guard became curious about the shirt apparently lying loose in the field, the game would be up. Finally, on February 9, Rose announced that they were ready. They would break out at seven that evening. To cover the escape, other prisoners agreed to stage a loud and boisterous musical show.

Rose and Hamilton led the first contingent

Federal captives peer from the windows of Richmond's Libby Prison. In February 1864, more than 100 men escaped through a tunnel under the lot in the foreground.

The Libby Prison escape route is diagramed at left. By cutting through the back of a fireplace in the kitchen (6), the inmates gained access to the cellar (11); they then burrowed under the vacant lot (13) until their tunnel (15) emerged in a shed (17) that gave access to an adjacent building (19).

through the tunnel, each man following close on the heels of the one in front of him. Rose broke ground exactly where he expected to, just on the safe side of the fence, and quickly escapees began fanning out in the dark on Richmond's streets. Meanwhile, the inmates covering the escape looked out from the prison's upper-story windows and saw the men break free. Carried away by enthusiasm, many abandoned their musicale and started to the basement to join the escape. Before dawn, six colonels, six lieutenant colonels, seven majors, 32 captains, and 58 lieutenants had emerged from the hole to disappear into the night.

The men walked calmly toward the homes of known Unionists in the city, or they headed north and east toward Federal lines. Many passed through Richmond's gaslit streets, wrote Hobart, "without creating a suspicion as to our real character." Not until morning roll call at the prison was their absence discovered. "When the rebel officers counted the men they found one hundred and nine too few," wrote one prisoner who had stayed behind. "In a twinkling, church bells were ringing, cavalrymen were out with horns blaring, and all hounds obtainable were yelping."

Rose did not reach safety. He and 47 others were soon recaptured (the enterprising colonel would spend many days in solitary confinement). Two other officers drowned attempting to swim across swollen streams. Yet the remaining 59 made it back to their own lines.

Despite inspirational examples like the Libby Prison breakout, few prisoners could seriously aspire to escape. After only a little time in confinement, a man's physique was hardly up to the rigors of a prolonged flight.

Nor were his spirits. Describing the psychological deterioration of men in camp, a New Yorker at a prison compound in Savannah, Georgia, wrote of inmates who sat "moping for hours with a look of utter dejection, their elbow upon their knee, and their chin resting upon their hand, their eyes having a vacant, far-away look." Such prisoners languished through the months and years in places that were little heard of before the War, but which soon became storied sites of hardship, suffering and death.

"If there was a hell on earth," wrote a Texan, "Elmira prison was that hell." No compound struck a deeper chill into the hearts of Confederate soldiers. Opened in July 1864, it occupied 30 acres along New York's Chemung River. Flooding of the river soon left a stagnant pool 40 feet wide and three to five feet deep in the center of the compound. Into the muck went garbage and thousands of gallons of camp sewage. The pond rapidly became a cesspool, a "festering mass of corruption" whose "pestilential odors" caused men who breathed them to vomit. Despite the health hazard that the pond presented, several months elapsed before William Hoffman gave the prisoners permission to build their own drainage ditch.

Other discomforts at Elmira went unremedied. After six months, the cheap, green lumber Hoffman had authorized for the barracks began to split and crack. Lacking foundations, the barracks' floors were constantly cold and damp. And despite indications that the camp could expect 10,000 or more prisoners, preparations were made for barely half that. Only six weeks after Elmira opened, the barracks housed 9,600 Rebels. As new prisoners arrived, they were crammed into hastily erected tents. And

Two Federal lieutenants who escaped from the prison camp at Columbia, South Carolina, on November 29, 1864, appear tattered but triumphant shortly after reaching the Union lines at Loudon, Tennessee, 225 miles distant, on February 6, 1865. The officers used their hickory walking sticks to fend off plantation guard dogs.

when tents ran out, some prisoners had to sleep out in the open.

Winter came early that year. The one stove allotted per barracks was woefully inadequate to warm the 200 inhabitants. Every morning, recalled a Confederate cavalryman, "the men crawled out of their bunks shivering and half frozen, when a scuffle, and frequently a fight, for a place by the fire occurred. God help the sick or the weak, as they were literally left out in the cold."

In December 1864, it was reported that more than 1,600 of the prisoners at Elmira had inadequate clothing and no blankets. The inmates stood ankle-deep in snow that winter to answer morning roll call. Small wonder that for six of its 12 months of existence, Elmira led all Northern prisons in its death rate, an average of 10 a day. Diarrhea and dysentery prostrated the men in droves. In September 1864 scurvy afflicted fully one

fifth of the camp. An inspector found the men "pale and emaciated, hollow-eyed and dispirited in every act and movement."

The commandant himself warned his superiors that if the rate of sickness continued at such levels, everyone in the camp would soon be dead. His prediction was not borne out, but the final tally was grim enough. By the time Elmira closed its gates in the summer of 1865, more than 12,000 Confederates had dwelt within its stockade; almost 3,000 of them had died there.

Yet even Elmira would pale in comparison with the place that came to epitomize the evils of the prison camps. Early in 1864, with the Confederate prisons in Virginia filled beyond capacity and Federal forces advancing slowly through the state, General Winder began transferring most of the Federal enlisted men to a new prison in a more secure area where provisions were thought to be more abundant. Built on an isolated plain in south central Georgia, the compound was called Camp Sumter to commemorate the Confederate victory at Charleston, but soon it became known by the name of a nearby settlement, Andersonville.

At Andersonville, the difficulty of acquiring tools and lumber proved so acute that the only structures to be erected were shanties used for headquarters, cookhouses and bakeries. The 27-acre camp was enclosed by a stockade fence. Fifteen feet inside of the perimeter wall was a built-in deterrent to escape, an ominous cordon called the "dead line." It consisted of short wooden posts topped with a single rail. The frail structure was no physical barrier, but the prisoners were forewarned of the consequences of venturing beyond it: Guards were instructed to

Federal prisoners amid a sea of ragged shelters swelter in the August heat at Andersonville, Georgia, in 1864. The trench latrine runs alongside the stream from which the men drew bathing and drinking water.

call out a warning to a prisoner who approached the line; if he stepped over it, the guards would open fire. During Andersonville's brief existence, many men would be killed beyond the dead line.

The first prisoners arrived in February 1864 with the camp still unfinished, and before arrangements could be made for the new arrivals, more poured into the stockade. There were 7,500 inmates by March, 15,000 by May, and 29,000 by July. The prisoners had to provide their own shelter; most of them fashioned rude lean-tos out of blankets, clothing, sticks and whatever else they could find or scavenge. Some dug holes in the ground and covered them with blankets. There were 33,000 Federals crammed into the compound by August 1864, and each inmate had little more than enough space to lie down in. Incredibly, only four cities in the Confederacy had a greater population than Andersonville Prison.

The commandant of Andersonville was Captain Henry Wirz. A native of Switzerland, he had served nine years in various European armies, absorbing their doctrines of rigid organization and strict discipline, before becoming a physician in Louisiana. After joining the Confederate Army, he was seriously wounded at Seven Pines in 1862; the injury left one arm permanently useless and Wirz himself in almost constant pain. His accent was pronounced, and it grew thicker when he was angered, which was often. The Federals who came under his command after he became a prison commandant took an instant dislike to him. One prisoner described him as "a most savage looking man, and who was as brutal as his looks would seem to indicate."

Wirz was accused of every sort of atroc-

ity. A Massachusetts artilleryman asserted that when he arrived at Andersonville, Wirz forced him and the other prisoners in his unit to stand in line while he strolled back and forth in front of them waving a huge pistol and shouting, "What'd you come down here for? First got-dam man that falls out of line I blow him to hell. I make you wish you stay at home!"

His accent, his foreign birth, his temper, and the miserable conditions of his camp all combined to make Wirz a hated and marked man. Many a prisoner under his rule vowed to take vengeance on him if ever the War came to an end.

For all his faults, Wirz could hardly be held accountable for the acute shortages at Andersonville of every necessity: food, clothing, shelter and medical care. The assistant quartermaster there complained that he had to bury the dead without coffins for want of wood. And the remoteness of Andersonville, combined with the critical food shortages then plaguing most of the South, reduced rations to the point where the men were on the brink of starvation.

The crowding produced massive pollution. Bisecting the compound was a small stream called, perversely, Sweet Water Branch. Andersonville's chief source of wa-

Andersonville prisoners gather en masse at a distribution point in August 1864 to receive their rations. According to an inmate, the daily food allotment generally consisted of a teaspoon of salt and three table-spoons of beans, along with half a pint of unsifted corn meal that "cut and inflamed the stomach and intestines like handfuls of pounded glass."

Workers at Andersonville bury the victims of disease, starvation and exposure in a shallow mass grave north of the stockade. In August 1864 the death rate exceeded 100 men per day.

ter, the stream also served as a garbage dump for the hospital and cookhouse. Seepage from the latrine, built parallel to the stream, added to the filth, in which mosquitoes, flies, lice and fleas bred copiously.

By May 1864, fifty per cent of the prison's inmates were reported sick. Most of the men who came to Andersonville were already weakened from months or years of confinement in other prisons in Virginia. In fact, Andersonville was more a vast, ill-organized and thoroughly inadequate hospital than a prison. It needed not guards, but doctors and medicines. The lack of medical care was the chief reason for the dreadfully high mortality rate. Some 13,000 men died at Andersonville in less than a year. In one awful day, the death toll from disease, malnutrition and other causes came to 127 men — or one death every 11 minutes.

For the men at Andersonville and the other prison camps, the ordeal eventually ended, one way or another. The prisoner exchange system was finally reactivated early in 1865, but by then it made little difference. Advancing Federal armies were freeing prisoners throughout the South, and Winder and his associates, seeing little else to do, finally ceased trying to hold on to their remaining charges. Instead, they simply began paroling them and sending them back to Federal lines. Winder himself, aged and worn down by the cares and burdens of his office, died on February 7, 1865, and perhaps it was just as well. Had he survived the War, he would surely have faced a Federal tribunal.

With the coming of peace, prison doors everywhere opened, but the bitterness stored up during years of confinement was not to be erased by the coming of peace. Too

Last Voyage of the Sultana

On April 24, 1865, the side-wheeler *Sultana* departed Vicksburg on the Mississippi River, bound for Cairo, Illinois, with 2,100 freed Federal prisoners of war crammed onto her decks. It was a risky undertaking. The *Sultana* was designed to carry only 376 passengers and crew. To make things worse, one of her boilers began leaking and twice required repairs as the ship churned north against a powerful, flood-stage current.

Scarcely an hour after the *Sultana* left Memphis astern early on the morning of April 27, catastrophe struck: The patched boiler burst in a shuddering explosion that ripped through the ship and shot a pillar of orange flame into the sky. Men asleep on the boiler deck were hurled into the air; they fell back into scalding water on deck or landed in the cold, swirling Mississippi.

Coals from the ruptured furnaces helped spread the fire. One soldier saw men "tossing their arms wildly in the air, and rushing pell-mell" over the guardrail into the river. Another recalled the passengers "jumping from all parts of the boat into the water, until it seemed black with men." Hundreds of prisoners, enfeebled by disease and starvation, lacked the strength to swim ashore; others simply did not know how.

The *Sultana* became a floating inferno. "The whole heavens seemed to be lighted up by the conflagration," wrote a survivor. Yet still some hung on. The men who feared the water more than the fire clung to the rails, another witness reported, "until they were singed off like flies. Shrieks and cries for mercy were all that could be heard, and that awful morning reminded me of the stories of doomsday of my childhood." By 3:15 a.m., no one on board the *Sultana* was alive. The ship continued to burn for another five hours before sinking in a plume of smoke and hissing steam.

When dawn came, rescue craft picked up men clutching onto anything that would float — cabin furniture, hay bales, mule carcasses, even human bodies. Truman Smith of the 8th Michigan Cavalry spotted four men riding downstream on the roots of a tree; they were singing "The Star-Spangled Banner."

Over the next few weeks, bodies were fished from the river as far away as Helena, Arkansas, 120 miles downstream. The disaster had claimed some 1,700 victims — men who had survived the horrors of Confederate prison camps only to perish within a two-day journey of their Midwestern homes.

Released Federal prisoners throng the decks of the steamer *Sultana* at Helena, Arkansas, on April 26, 1865 — 19 hours before the ship blew up.

many had died. Altogether, about 211,000 Union troops had been captured during the War, and 194,000 of them went into Southern prisons. There, 30,000 of them — more than 15 per cent — died. Of the 214,000 Confederates sent north to Union prisons, about 26,000 died, or roughly 12 per cent. Now that the War was over, the vanquished Southerners could do nothing but try to forget the horrors of prison — although they were unforgettable. The victors, however, wanted revenge.

The publicity and propaganda associated with Andersonville at the end of the War made it inevitable that someone pay a price for what had happened there. Winder was dead, and that left only Wirz to take the blame. In May 1865, Federal authorities arrested him and took him to Washington, where he appeared before a military tribunal. The commandant of Andersonville was accused of conspiring "to injure the health and destroy the lives of soldiers in the military service of the United States." More serious than that, he was charged with "murder in violation of the laws and customs of war."

Wirz's trial that summer was flawed. Witness after witness gave testimony of the commandant's misdeeds, but some of it was blatantly contrived. Prosecutors manipulated evidence to suit their case, and the defense was denied motion after motion. The press called Wirz "the Andersonville savage," "the inhuman wretch," "the infamous Captain." Wirz repeatedly protested that he was merely a soldier carrying out orders in a dire situation. One of his own prisoners would later concede: "He might have commanded a company well, and possibly a regiment, but thirty thousand men got away from

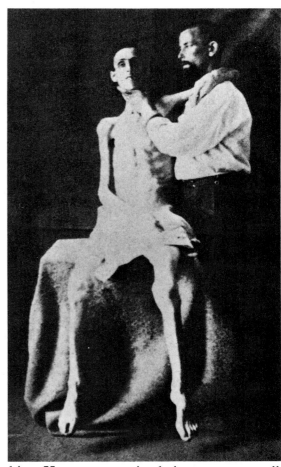

him. He was at sea in their management."

The outcome of Wirz's trial was never in doubt from the moment it began. Found guilty on all charges, Wirz calmly mounted the gallows on November 10, 1865, amid an almost carnival atmosphere. Reporters flocked around the scaffold in the yard of the Old Capitol Prison. Soldiers lining the walls chanted over and over again, "Andersonville, Andersonville," until the trap dropped and Wirz was dead. In a sense, he was the last casualty of the prison camps. But the injuries to body and spirit inflicted in those places would long be felt by the men who survived.

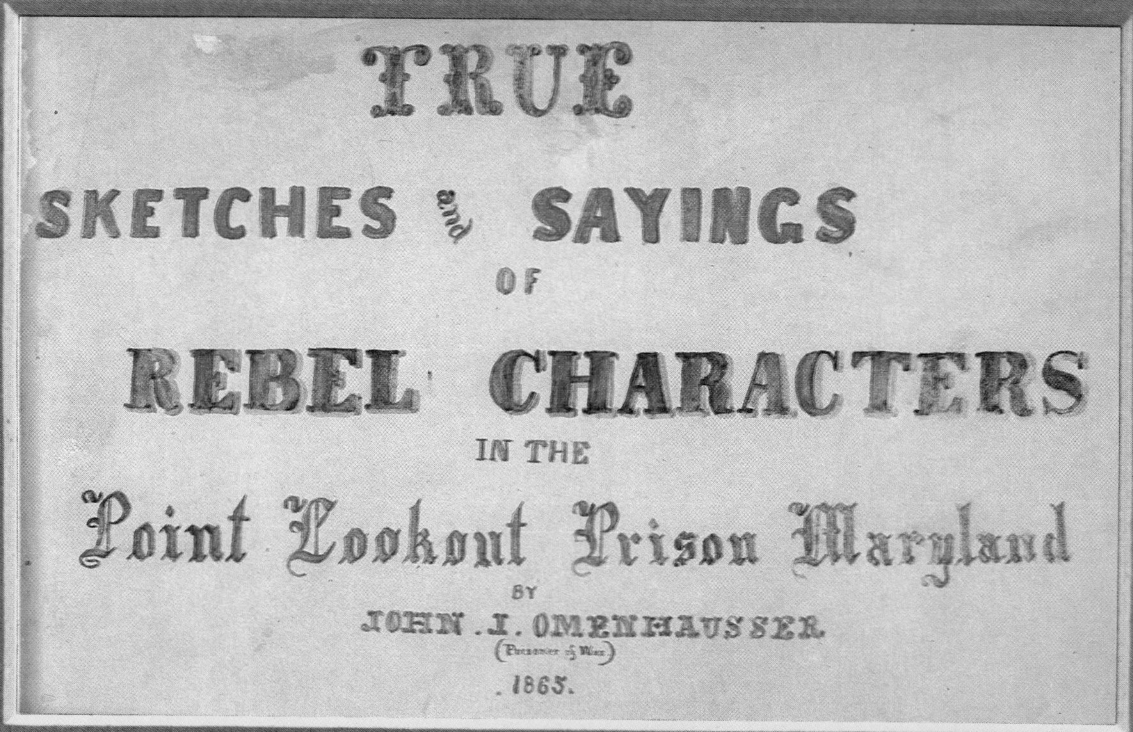

TRUE
SKETCHES and SAYINGS
OF
REBEL CHARACTERS
IN THE
Point Lookout Prison Maryland
BY
JOHN J. OMENHAUSSER
(Prisoner of War)
1865.

After Private John T. Omenhausser of the 46th Virginia Infantry was captured near Petersburg on June 16, 1864, and sent to the Federal prisoner-of-war camp at Point Lookout, Maryland, he turned to sketching to fill the long hours of incarceration. Point Lookout, situated on a barren, swampy bit of land at the mouth of the Potomac River, packed as many as 20,000 inmates into an enclosure intended for half that number. The prisoners lacked sufficient drinking water, food and shelter, and 3,000 Confederates perished there during the War. But Omenhausser's crudely captioned drawings, 14 of which are reproduced here, portray the prisoners enduring their circumstances with pluck and surprising humor. In the last sketch on these pages, a prisoner swears an oath of allegiance to the Union to gain his release — precisely what Omenhausser did on June 9, 1865, after spending a year at Point Lookout.

No 1. Boys thats my rat if you kill him, he been eating my bread for the Past three days.

No 2. Dont let that rat get away, peel your foot on him.

No 3. Let him alone I'll get him.

No 4. Hello Sam! what are you going to do with them rats, are you going to eat them?!

5 Certainly I am they are as good as squirl, and they make a fellows rations hold out. — go and get your bread and come and take dinner with me.

No 1. Halt! Der white man phar you gwoine?

2 I'm going to thirwak.

1 Whats dat?

2 I'm going to piss.

1 Dar you's done toll ten tale's about it, now double quick back to your tent

No 3. Git down on your knees and pray for Abram Lincoln.

4. Oh Lord bless President Lincoln

3 Now pray for de United States.

4. Oh Lord! bless the army and navy of the United States.

3. Now pray for de colored people.

4. Oh Lord have mercy on the niggers, no I mean on the colored people and deliver them from bondage.

The Reb who has Friends at the North.   The Reb who has no friends at the North.

Nº 1. Some Rebs say they don't get enough to eat, but I don't believe them.
I always have plenty. I wonder if the Baltimore boat has arrived yet
I expect a box of eatables.

" 2. You can sweeten your coffee to suit your self.

Nº 3. This is my whole days ration, and it won't do to eat it all at
once or I won't have any thing for supper.

" 4. My Bread ration was stopt to-day for missing roll call, I
beleive I'll lay down and sleep off my appetite.

Guards buying rings from Rebels.

Nº 1. Look at that d—m nigger getting all the best rings, nigger why don't you
look out for the Officer of the day.

" 2. D—m de Officer of day, nigger how you like dem, eh.

" 3. Sentinel don't you want to buy some nice tobacco?

" 4. Here's a ring you may have for fifty cents.

Nº 5. Here's a ring I'll warrant to be silver.

" 6. Here's a nice ring you may have for twenty five cents.

" 7. I wonder if I couldn't sell them darkies this brass ring for gold.

" 8. Warrant it gold, and they'll buy it, they won't know you from the
man in the moon.

An Every day Scene at the Fourth Division Pump.

Nº 1. I bet I'll get some water, or have a fight.

" 2. I've been two hours getting this cup full.

" 3. A fellow with a canteen dont stand no show.

" 4. I had hold of the handle first, its my next turn.

Nº 5. Let go the handle or I'll break your head.

" 6. You call'd one a liar did you, take that.

" 7. Never mind I'll be even with you yet.

POINT LOOKOUT MD.

The Reb that never saw a crab   Cook'd Crabs

Nº 1. Mister just smell this bugs breath its the sweetest thing you ever smelt.

" 2. Make the damm thing let loose, or I'll smash his brains out.

" 3. Ha! Ha! Ha! I wonder if that feller will smell any more bugs.

Nº 4 Mister I'll give you a big chew tobacco for this feller.

" 5. Mister are them things good to eat?

" 6. Yes does you think I'd sell any thing that wasn't good to eat.

No. 1. Jim! how do you like the Jewelry and Uniform the Major made us a present of

" 2. If we had'nt been a pair of fools, we'd never got in this fix.

" 3. Yeah! Yeah! Barnum ought to have them fellers in his show, I think they'd pay well.

No. 4. I don't see what that nigger sees to laugh at, I don't think this is so very amusing.

" 5. If I'd catch any damn Reb trying to get my box tobacco, I'd break his blame head for him.

No. 1. Don't these mellons put me in mind of home and my Sister Jane.

No. 2. Mister give me the Rhine, I want to make Pickels

No. 3. He don't want them to make pickles, he wants them to eat,

No. 4. Mister how many apples will you give me for this fine tooth comb. its not been used much

No. 5. Go to the devil with your fine tooth Louera trap, and make good use of it. I don't want it.

Chuck luck.   Keeno or Lotto.

Nº 1. I'll bet my last chew on the ace.

" 2. Heres the place to bet your Greenbacks, Confeds, tobacco or crackers

" 3. Mister can I bet this cracker against a chew tobacco.

Nº 4. Thirty nine!

" 5. Keeno on the bottom line

" 6 Why did'nt you call out thirty eight, I had two show 3.

Nº 7. I have lost all my Tobacco and have not won a single pot?

Washing

Nº 1. Greybacks like warm, I wonder if they like warm water.

" 2. If there are any more Greybacks in here I'll be dog'd if I don't make them suffer.

Nº 3. Bob why don't you holler out and let the fellers know we take in Washing?

Nº 4. Heres the place to have your washing done, two peices for five cents.

Nº 1. Why in the devil dont you make your biscuits larger, I can eat three dozen of them, and not half try.

" 2. Mister how many biscuits will you give me for this bit of bacon?

" 3 Heres your hot biscuits, five, and molasses to go with them for fivets.

Nº 4. It makes a fellow feel hungry, to come out here and see so many good thing, and so many to buy them.

" 5 I cant see, why they wont let a fellow cook in camp.

" 6. Heres your good Dixie Tobacco.

POINT LOOKOUT MARYLAND.

CAMP INSPECTION.

Nº 1 Just see what suffering, Jeff Davis has brought on these poor fellows.

Nº 2. You need not stick your foot out in that way, I can see them.

" 3. Front rank! Left dress.

CONFEDERATE VARIETY'S.

POINT LOOKOUT MARYLAND

Nº 1. Do you wish to take the Oath.   Nº 2. I Do in the cool.

ROLL OFFICE

REBELS SWALLOWING THE OATH.

Tests of Honor

The mettle of a Civil War soldier was tested often and in countless ways. He was expected to tolerate the boredom of drill and the monotony and discomfort of life in camp or on the march. His lot was to suffer stoically through debilitating illnesses, often far from the minimal comforts of hospital or sickbed. He coped with homesickness, loneliness and deep anxiety for the welfare of those family members he was compelled to leave behind. And sooner or later, the soldier could expect to meet the supreme test — battle.

Although fighting typically consumed a minute amount of a soldier's time in service, this prospect was never far from a man's mind. It was a trial deeply dreaded, not only because combat might maim him or end his life, but also because most soldiers were afraid that they might turn coward and bring shame upon themselves, their families and their regiments. "I have a mortal fear of the battlefield," a Massachusetts lad confessed before his first taste of fighting in 1863. "I am afraid that the groans of the wounded and dying will make me shake; nevertheless, I hope and trust that strength will be given me to stand up and do my duty."

To do one's duty, in situations both routine and extraordinary, was the job of the common soldier. Many needed nothing beyond their own inner resources to endure the pressures of army life. Others relied on comradeship or the example of outstanding leaders. Still others drew the necessary solace and strength from the teachings of their reli-

gion. They came, after all, from a society in which religion was a part of everyday life, and in which church affiliation was as much a part of one's identity as nationality, place of residence or trade. Far from home, soldiers often turned to their regimental chaplains for emotional support in times of peril.

Although chaplains had no authority to give orders, these uniformed men of God were technically officers and therefore relatively well paid — $80 per month in the Confederacy and $100 per month in the Union. In the South, they were usually elected by the troops of a regiment and commissioned by President Jefferson Davis. Federal Army chaplains, on the other hand, were chosen by a regiment's officers or appointed by the state Governor. In either case, the chaplain reported to the colonel of his regiment.

But the commanding officer seldom evidenced much interest in the chaplain's duties or in providing him the means to perform them. A Rhode Island cleric, Frederic Denison, complained that the chaplain had "no appointment or recognized place on a march, in a bivouac, or in a line of battle; he was a supernumerary, a kind of fifth wheel to a coach, being in place nowhere and out of place everywhere." Some officers did not want a clergyman around, lest he provide what one Federal chaplain called "a standing reproof" of their "wicked conduct."

In spite of their ambiguous role, many chaplains made a place for themselves in the daily life of the soldiers, taking as a

Dozens of sentimental songs were published during the Civil War, but none was more popular than "Just before the Battle, Mother," with its tearful refrain: "Farewell mother, you may never press me to your heart again." Sold in the form of this song sheet, elaborately decorated with illustrations of other ballads by composer George Root, it touched the hearts of millions.

Father Thomas H. Mooney, a chaplain from New York City, says Mass for the Irish 69th New York in camp at Arlington, Virginia, before the Battle of Bull Run in 1861. To raise the morale of the 69th and show that God was on its side, Mooney christened a cannon — an act that was popular with the troops, but that earned him a rebuke from his bishop.

primary duty the counseling and consoling of the troubled, the ill and wounded, and those facing death. Beyond that, the man of God often became a camp factotum, distributing religious literature, running a camp library, sending accounts of the soldiers to their local newspapers, and begging supplies from the home congregations. He wrote and read letters for the illiterate men, and frequently took charge of the incoming and outgoing mail. Chaplain Richard Eddy of the 60th New York personally processed 3,063 letters for his regiment during the month of March 1862.

Such chaplains earned the love and respect of the men they served. The surgeon of the 42nd Mississippi remembered that Chaplain Thomas Witherspoon was "every man's friend, and the oldest and youngest soldier felt no hesitation in approaching him in time of trouble. He was a devout, humble, hopeful Christian, and his daily walk and example was a benediction to his brigade."

The few Jewish clergymen in uniform maintained the same spirit of service, often in the face of galling prejudice. A general order of May 4, 1861, required that a chaplain in the Federal Army be "a regularly ordained minister of some Christian denomination." As a result, one rabbi serving as a chaplain was compelled to resign, and another was denied his appointment. The protests that resulted soon persuaded the War Department to drop the discriminatory requirement.

The work of the clerics in the field was supplemented in both Armies by large civilian organizations. The United States Christian Commission, which was sponsored by the Young Men's Christian Association, raised more than four million dollars in do-nations in the North for printing and distributing religious pamphlets and materials. In 1864 alone, the commission dispensed to Federal soldiers 569,700 Bibles, 4,815,000 hymnals and psalm books, and 13,681,000 pages of religious tracts. In the South, individual denominations, along with Bible societies and other groups, raised money to purchase religious materials for Confederate troops. In the war-ravaged economy of the Confederacy, however, the effort proved increasingly difficult.

Worse, there were never enough chaplains to go around. In June 1862, after a year of war, the Federal Army had only 395 chaplains for its 676 regiments, and 42 of those men were absent, some without leave. Yet the Union was better off than the Confederacy; in 1863 fully one half of Confederate regiments were without chaplains. Prosperous civilian clerics were reluctant to give up their positions for the risks and lower pay of army life. Many of the chaplains who did serve had been unable to find churches in civilian life.

A few were outright rogues. A Wisconsin chaplain made himself notorious by boarding in a Washington brothel while his regiment was in the field. The chaplain of the 127th New York actually charged the men a penny for every letter he handled for them, prompting the men to refer to him contemptuously as "One Cent by God." Private Thomas E. Caffey, an Englishman serving in the 18th Mississippi, was scathingly critical of the chaplains he encountered, labeling them "a race of long-jawed, loud-mouthed ranters, termed for courtesy's sake ministers of the Gospel." They were, he concluded, "terribly valiant in words, and offensively loquacious upon every topic of life, save men's salvation."

But the presence of a few misfits could not quench the thirst for religious affirmation shared by many Civil War soldiers. From time to time, this yearning manifested itself in revivals — emotional gatherings conducted by evangelists specializing in mass conversions and awakenings. These campaigns were fewer and of shorter duration among the Federals than among the beleaguered Confederates.

A great revival swept through Lee's Army of Northern Virginia in 1863. "The gathering each night of bronzed and grizzly warriors devoutly worshipping was a wonderful picture in the army," wrote John Worsham of the 21st Virginia, "and when some old familiar hymn was given out, those thousands of warriors would make hill and dell ring." One exhilarated clergyman, setting aside the jealousies of interdenominational rivalry, boasted that "we had a Presbyterian sermon, introduced by Baptist services, under the direction of a Methodist chaplain,

in an Episcopal church. Was not that a beautiful solution of the vexed problem of Christian union?" A visitor to the Army of Northern Virginia offered a lyrical account of the revival's effect: "Pentecostal fire lights the camp, and the hosts of armed men sleep beneath the wings of angels rejoicing over many sinners that have repented."

The fervid exhortations by chaplains and evangelists produced hundreds of conversions and affirmations of faith. Although the movement was interrupted that summer by the Gettysburg and Vicksburg Campaigns, many Confederates saw in the dire results of those clashes the hand of God, and they determined to pray even harder and strive for greater righteousness. Their resolve spurred the revival on until it reached from the Atlantic to the Mississippi and beyond, and swept up more than 100,000 souls.

A less dramatic but more regular expression of devotion was the Sunday afternoon worship service conducted by most chap-

Volunteers of the U.S. Christian Commission, a Protestant charity, gather before tents open to the troops at a Federal encampment near Germantown, Virginia, in 1863. These self-styled "ambassadors for Jesus" distributed Bibles and hymn books, held prayer meetings, gave away stationery and postage stamps, and offered lonely soldiers free coffee, hot soup and a sympathetic ear.

lains. It was a simple affair, consisting of a couple of hymns, a scripture reading, and then the sermon. Chaplains often based their talks upon martial passages from the Bible, consoling the men in time of defeat by remembering the sufferings of the Israelites, and reminding them in days of victory that all glory belongs to the Almighty.

A few clerics made no attempt to tailor their remarks to the situation. At least one brought into the army copies of the sermons he had delivered in civilian life. "The preacher took an old piece of faded yellow manuscript and began the sermon," Lieutenant Samuel Craig complained, "discussed infant baptism and closed with an earnest appeal, touchingly eloquent, to mothers! I'm sure there wasn't a mother in the regiment,"

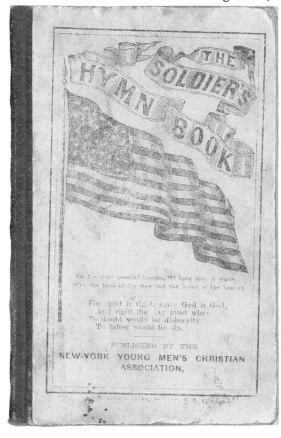

In the words of its preface, this patriotic hymnal, issued in 1861 by the newly founded Young Men's Christian Association, was printed for Federal volunteers "who so suddenly and in such large numbers have taken up arms for the defense of our country." Many soldiers carried the hymnals with them into battle.

Craig went on, "and not more than two or three infants."

Traditional hellfire-and-brimstone sermons, laced with dreadful threats of eternal damnation, enjoyed little popularity. A Union chaplain who was fond of issuing frequent warnings that the end was near came to be known as "Death on a Pale Horse." A Wisconsin colonel expressed the attitude of many officers: "I don't want any more of that doctrine preached in this regiment. Every one of my boys who fall fighting this great battle of liberty is going to Heaven, and I won't allow any other principle to be promulgated to them while I command this regiment."

Attendance at services was generally voluntary, and the men were easily distracted. While a new Confederate chaplain was delivering his first sermon to a regiment of Kentuckians, his entire audience wandered off to look at a newly arrived cannon. Profoundly discouraged, the minister left too — and never returned.

On other occasions soldiers proved rigidly devout at the services. Outside Richmond, prior to one of the Seven Days' Battles in 1862, the Reverend Joseph Clay Stiles was addressing several companies of Virginians and South Carolinians gathered at an advance position. With the men on their knees, eyes fervently closed, Stiles had just begun his prayer when an enemy battery sent two or three shells whistling over their heads.

Stiles's son, who was among the worshippers, wrote later that "faith and devotion were not strong enough to prevent my opening my eyes and glancing around." Others kept their eyes shut, refusing to be distracted. But when the shells began to come closer, those still at prayer "felt it would be wise and

Making Legends of Regimental Mascots

The morale of the rank and file was always elevated by the presence of pets. The soldiers enjoyed playing with the animals and were eager to endow their mascots with larger-than-life attributes. The 12th Wisconsin Volunteers had a tame bear that marched with them all the way to Missouri, and even the lowliest stray dog could become the stuff of regimental legend.

When the volunteer firemen of Niagara, Pennsylvania, enlisted en masse in their state's 102nd Infantry, they brought along a doleful black-and-white bull terrier named Jack *(left)*, whose subsequent career spanned nearly all the regiment's battles in Virginia and Maryland. It was said that he understood bugle calls and obeyed only the men of his regiment, and that after a battle he searched out the wounded and the dead.

According to a tongue-in-cheek account by the regimental historian, Jack was severely wounded at Malvern Hill. Captured by the enemy at Savage's Station, he managed to escape. His barking was heard above the din at Antietam, and he was wounded again at Fredericksburg. At Salem Church, he was taken prisoner a second time. Six months later, according to the chronicler, he was exchanged for a Confederate soldier at Belle Isle.

Rejoining his unit, Jack went south under General Grant through the bloody campaigns of the Wilderness and Spotsylvania and the siege of Petersburg. Alas, he did not witness the final victory at Appomattox: In 1864, a few days after his comrades gave him a beautiful silver collar worth $75, he disappeared forever, apparently the victim of a robber.

Many other dogs won fame for their apocryphal exploits on the battlefield. Major, a lion-hearted mutt who accompanied the 10th Maine — later reorganized as the 29th Maine — was said to demonstrate his mettle by snapping at Confederate Minié balls in flight. Eventually he caught one — and perished.

Then there was the dog who entered legend at Antietam. During the battle, the beast's owner, Captain Werner von Bachelle of the 6th Wisconsin, fell mor-

Two soldiers of the 29th Maine have their portrait made with Major, their regimental mascot. When the unit was sent to Louisiana, Major went along; he lost his life at Sabine Cross Roads during the Red River Campaign in 1864.

Below, Old Abe the eagle poses atop his perch with his handlers, the color guard of the 8th Wisconsin. Lithographs of the famous Federal mascot (*right*) were produced by the thousands and sold to benefit the Chicago Sanitary Commission's Fair in 1865.

tally wounded. As the story went, the pet stayed at von Bachelle's side and the next morning was found atop the corpse, shot dead while defending his master.

The most celebrated of all Civil War mascots was the 8th Wisconsin's eagle, Old Abe (*right*), who was carried into battle tethered to a perch alongside the regimental colors. During the War, he had no fewer than six bearers, three of whom were shot from under him. When the regiment was mustered out in 1864, Old Abe was sent to the state capital at Madison where he resided until the end of his days in a special cage at the Statehouse. Hundreds of photographs were made of him both during and after the War, and by the time he died in 1881, he had become for millions a symbol of American courage and fortitude.

well," wrote the younger Stiles, "to supplement the protection of heaven by the trees and stumps of earth, if they could find them, and so they were actually groping for them with arms wide extended but eyes tight closed, and still on their knees."

Although chaplains were not required to take part in any military operations, many of them did nevertheless. Confederate Chaplain William E. Wiatt sometimes carried the rifles of weak or ailing soldiers on the march; once the exertion so sapped his strength that he had to remain in bed for a week afterward.

Some went into battle with their men. According to the colonel of the 94th Illinois, Chaplain R. E. Guthrie was on the field throughout the entire engagement at Prairie Grove, Arkansas, in 1862, calling on the men to "trust in God, do their duty, and fire low." On another occasion, Colonel John Beatty of the 3rd Ohio recalled seeing a "fighting parson who had two revolvers and a hatchet in his belt and appeared more like a firebrand of war than a minister of peace."

A number of chaplains, including at least 11 on the Union side, died of wounds received in combat. One of the casualties was the Reverend Arthur B. Fuller, who had been discharged from the 16th Massachusetts in December 1862 just before the Battle of Fredericksburg, but chose to remain with his friends a little longer. Rifle in hand, he was killed as the Federals moved through the town. A Confederate casualty was claimed at Jonesboro, Georgia, on August 31, 1864, when a priest by the name of Blemill went into battle with the 4th Kentucky. As the regiment was withdrawing from the fight, Blemill was seen bending over a dying man, hands lifted in prayer. The next moment a cannonball decapitated the priest.

Executive Department of Alabama,
MONTGOMERY, OCTOBER 2d, 1864.

TO ALABAMA SOLDIERS
ABSENT FROM THEIR COMMANDS:

Many of you have, doubtless, remained at home after the expiration of your furloughs, without the intention to desert the cause of your country, and you have failed to return to your Commands for fear of the penalty to which you may be subjected. Many of you have left your Commands without leave, under the mistaken notion that the highest duty required you to provide sustenance and protection to your families. Some have been prompted to leave by one motive and some by others. Very few, I am persuaded, have left with the intent to abandon the cause of the South.

I have received letters from several expressing sorrow for their past neglect of duty, and a wish to return to their Commands, if any assurance could be given that they would not receive the extreme penalty of the law.

At this time, our cause needs all men able and willing to bear arms in its defense. The best recommendation to those who have, heretofore, neglected their duty is a prompt acknowledgement of their fault, manifested by their prompt return to duty. But that there may be no obstacle in the way of those who really desire to serve their country, I am authorized to say, that **ALL WHO WILL**, WITHOUT DELAY, **VOLUNTARILY** return to their Commands, will receive a lenient and merciful consideration; and that none, who so return within forty days from this date, will have the penalty of death inflicted on them.

I promise all, who will heed this appeal, to use my best exertions for their good.

T. H. WATTS,
Governor of Alabama.

Many chaplains did not shrink from risking their lives, for their patriotism ran just as high as that of their flocks. Chaplain Wiatt regarded it as "glorious to die the death of a Christian soldier and patriot."

As the conflict progressed, increasing numbers of soldiers, their resolve eroded by miseries and hazards of war, chose to desert. But many deserters took the step more out of concern for others than for themselves. Appeals from home for the man of the family to return exerted a powerful pull, especially in the South, where food was scarce and the wives of soldiers were struggling on their own, often under enemy occupation. A sense of futility infected the Confederacy late in the War. Early in 1865 a Confederate soldier in the trenches at Petersburg, Virginia, declared that it was useless "to conceal the truth any longer. Many of our people at home have become so demoralized that they write to their husbands, sons and brothers that desertion now is not dishonorable."

One of every seven Confederates would eventually desert. In the North, one of ten would do so. By 1864 the Union armies were heavily laced with conscripts, and men purchased with bounties, and few of them possessed sufficient patriotism to pass up an opportunity to escape, especially when the odds were 3 to 1 that an escape attempt would be successful.

From the outset, desertion was regarded as a serious threat to the welfare of both Armies. Top military officials, as well as Presidents Lincoln and Davis, attempted to lure the men back to their units with periodic impassioned pleas, proclamations of pardon and general amnesties. When this tactic achieved only limited success, the Armies pursued plans to deal sternly with offenders and dispense swift, uniform punishments.

But these intentions were soon frustrated by the large number of cases pending before courts-martial. The sudden mobilization of hundreds of thousands of men unused to army life naturally led to a raft of disciplinary cases. Courts-martial were not convened during an active campaign because officers at the front could not be spared to sit on them; during the delays, witnesses were often killed in battle before they could testify. Rather than wait for a trial that might never take place, many officers took military justice into their own hands.

As a result, punishments for desertion varied widely. Some offenders were discharged dishonorably — drummed out of the service. Others were given an indelible reminder of their sentence: a brand. With a red-hot iron, the letter *D* for "deserter" or *C* for "coward" was burned into the soldier's hip, hand, cheek or forehead. Many of the captured deserters were imprisoned, sometimes with rations restricted to bread and water. Others were sentenced to hard labor.

Despite such draconian measures, desertion had become epidemic by early 1865, and desperate commanders were reminded that one punishment allowed by military law was death. In the earlier years of the War, the death sentence was pronounced only rarely, and then it was generally commuted to long imprisonment. Although 80 Union deserters received the death sentence during a five-month period in 1863, only 21 of them were actually executed. But late in the War, the death sentence became far more frequent — in cases of rape, murder and espionage, as well as desertion.

When an execution was required, officers

In a delicately worded appeal, the Governor of Alabama promises lenient treatment to deserters from his state who return to their commands voluntarily within 40 days. By the last year of the War, the South was losing more men to desertion than to battle casualties.

ordered it done publicly, usually by firing squad. The condemned man was taken before his regiment — or sometimes before his entire corps — to hear the final reading of his sentence. After words of consolation from a chaplain, the man was usually blindfolded, and the deed was done. "It was hard to bear," wrote a witness to the execution of Frank McElhenny of the 24th Massachusetts. "Faces paled and hands shook which were not accustomed to show fear; and officers and men alike would have welcomed a call to battle in exchange for that terrible inaction in the sight of coming death."

Worse, the job was sometimes botched. The marksmanship of the average Civil War soldier was mediocre at best, and when soldiers were forced to shoot a defenseless comrade in cold blood, their aim could be terrible. Surely no military execution of the War was so badly bungled as that of Edward Latham and George Elliot of the 14th Connecticut, men who had been paid a bounty to enlist and then had deserted. Caught, convicted and sentenced to death, they were brought in an ambulance on September 18, 1863, to the open side of a square formed by an entire division of the II Corps near Culpeper Court House in Virginia. They sat on their coffins beside their open graves, heard a prayer and were blindfolded; then the officer in charge shook hands with the men. "The condemned men did not appear to manifest any concern," wrote Lieutenant Lemuel Jeffries, who observed the proceedings from the formation.

On command, the firing squad discharged a volley and Elliot fell back, apparently dead. But Latham was still sitting on his coffin; the bullets had missed him entirely. He "tore the handkerchief from his eyes and gazed around with a wild look," Jeffries recalled. Quickly the officer in charge sent two soldiers forward to take aim again from within six feet of the condemned man, who continued to sit on his coffin. The men pulled their triggers, but both guns failed to fire. "Many in the ranks now wished that Latham would get up and run for the woods," wrote Jeffries, "as the soldiers thought he had sufficiently risked his life." But the condemned man was paralyzed by fright or shock. The officer ran up to him, put his pistol to Latham's temple, and pulled the trigger. Nothing happened. "Now more than ever many wished he would get up and run," Jeffries wrote. But the officer tried again, and this time sent a ball into Latham's brain.

While this tragic farce had been going on, few had noticed the other man, Elliot, struggling to gain his feet. He had been shot painfully in the abdomen. "Blow my brains out!" he implored. The officer tried to comply, but he must have been shaken by the proceedings thus far, for even at point-blank range his aim was unsteady, and again Elliot was only wounded. It took two more rifle bullets in his chest to kill him; and still the distraught officer ordered two more rounds fired into the lifeless body, one of them from so close to Elliot's chest, Jeffries recorded, "that his clothes took fire from the powder flame."

The gruesome business over at last, the assembled troops were marched past the bodies of the slain so that, in Jeffries' words, "it might have a moral effect on them."

Despite the reluctance to use it early on, capital punishment was inflicted more often in the Civil War than it had been in all previous American wars combined. About 267 Federals were shot or hanged by order of

Standing behind his own coffin, a condemned Federal deserter (*above*) listens to a chaplain intone a final prayer while the men of the firing squad bow their uncovered heads. In the distance, troops from the deserter's division line up to watch. After the execution, cavalrymen troop past the body (*left*). As a final disgrace, deserters were often buried face down in unmarked graves.

courts-martial, about half of them for desertion. In the South the toll was probably comparable. "Shocking and solemn as such scenes were," concluded Private John D. Billings of Massachusetts, "I do not believe that the shooting of a deserter had any great deterring influence on the rank and file." There were simply too many opportunities to get away. "When a man's honor failed to hold him in the ranks, his exit from military life was easy enough."

Sooner or later, those whose sense of honor held them in the ranks would be called to battle. The onset of spring launched the campaign season. As the weather warmed, the troops received orders to break winter camp and prepare for the march. Rumors abounded — of military objectives and grand strategy — but the troops had little time to reflect on what might be in store for them, for there was much to be done. They filled up the baggage wagons with large tents, stoves, field forges, the camp's library, officers' furniture, and commissary equipment.

Rations were issued, usually a three-day supply to free the men from their commissary wagons and keep them ready for action. Yankee and Rebel alike often cooked and ate on the spot all the food they were given, reasoning that what they consumed they would not have to carry, and preferring, if fate so decreed, to go into battle on a full stomach. Finally, ordnance officers issued ammunition: 60 rounds of cartridges and percussion caps per man.

The regiment might march for days, even weeks, before encountering the enemy. On the day of battle, the fitful sleep of the troops was shattered before dawn by the insistent rattle of regimental drums sounding the "general," a signal to strike tents and assemble to move out. Eventually the marching men would hear the crack of musketry and the boom of cannon; then regiments would peel off from the main column and advance through the fields and woods to their place in the line of battle. For many, what followed was the hardest part of all — the waiting.

These were the moments when a man, though surrounded by thousands of comrades, felt entirely alone. Often he found all his senses heightened by his fear. Years afterward he might remember the bird song, the scent of the air, which flowers were in bloom, the sound of his heart beating. Perhaps he read a Bible if he had one, or whispered supplications. "Oh Lord," a young North Carolinian was heard to pray, "we have a mighty big fight down here, and a sight of trouble; and we hope, Lord, that you take a proper view of the matter, and give us the victory." But usually the concerns were more personal. A man thought of his past life, repented of his sins; he might pledge never to drink, gamble, curse or whore again, if only he might come through the day alive, and acquit himself well.

After the seemingly interminable wait at the edge of the battlefield, the order to advance was finally given, and the battle lines began moving, often under artillery bombardment. Each company was followed by the file closers, whose job it was to see that a soldier kept his place in the tight formation, 13 inches from the man in front and touching the elbow of the man on either side. The officers brought up the rear. Often the troops could see across an expanse of open ground the bristling line of guns and gleaming bayonets that marked the enemy line. The experienced men knew what lay ahead.

"To mass troops against the fire of a covered line is simply to devote them to destruction," lamented the Union's Major General John M. Schofield. "The greater the mass, the greater the loss — that is all." A man had to tap his deepest reservoirs of courage to face this prospect without flinching.

Some officers led by threat. Colonel Edward Cross of the 5th New Hampshire warned his men of the wages of cowardice before they entered the fray at Antietam: "Men, you are about to engage in battle. You have never disgraced your State; I hope you won't this time. If any man runs, I want the file closers to shoot him; if they don't, I shall myself. That's all I have to say."

Whether or not an officer had gained the respect of his men made an enormous difference in the way his troops behaved under fire. After the Wilson's Creek Campaign in late 1861, Sergeant William Watson of the 3rd Louisiana Volunteers recalled the influence that the regiment's commander, Colonel James McIntosh, had wielded in battle: "Col. M'Intosh, though very affable and pleasant in his manner, had nevertheless something so commanding in his deportment that he carried men with him in spite of themselves, and, although I would just as soon have been somewhere else than to be the first man marching up to that battery, yet I felt that I would rather die three times over than display the slightest fear under the eye of that man."

Not all soldiers overcame their fear. Some bolted, and did not hesitate to admit it. "If I hadent seen the fix I was in, and run like blazes, I would have been a goner by this time," a New Jersey man confessed after a battle in Georgia in 1864. A Maine soldier at Petersburg described his retreat during a Confederate attack: "They came in on us in 5 lines of batel, so sum of the boys say, but I did not stop to count. I limbered up for the rear as fast as legs cood cariery and that was pretty fast."

Yet the prospect of battle had the opposite effect on some men. "With your first shot you become a new man," remembered one veteran. "Personal safety is your least concern. Fear has no existence in your bosom. Hesitation gives way to an uncontrollable desire to rush into the thickest of the fight." Indeed, troops in the rear lines sometimes became so anxious to join the fray that they dashed through the ranks toward the front, causing severe disorder.

Charging against concentrated lines of the enemy, soldiers were seen to lean forward into the fire as if advancing into a hailstorm. All sensation blurred into an overwhelming surge of emotion. Major James Waddell of the 20th Georgia reported that at Second Bull Run he "carried into the fight over 100 men who were barefoot, many of whom left bloody foot-prints among the thorns and briars through which they rushed, with Spartan courage and really jubilant impetuosity, upon the serried ranks of the foe."

There were those whose anger and hatred for the enemy helped erase personal fears. When Private Oliver Norton of the 83rd Pennsylvania went into action at Gaines's Mill in 1862, he saw two friends fall in the first rush. "A kind of desperation seized me," Norton wrote. "I snatched a gun from the hands of a man who was shot through the head. Then I jumped over dead men with as little feeling as I would over a log. The feeling that was uppermost in my mind was a desire to kill as many rebels as I could. The loss of comrades maddened me."

Making Friends with the Enemy

In the lulls between battles, enemy troops at times established temporary bonds of friendship. The rival forces shared a common language and culture, of course, and a certain spirit of brotherhood persisted amid the hostilities.

One form of fraternization involved the trade of treasured items between the opposing ranks. Facing each other across a river, enemy pickets sometimes sent little hand-carved sailboats to the opposite shore, exchanging coffee that the Southern men craved for tobacco favored by the Federals. One of Robert E. Lee's soldiers remembered a day in the spring of 1862 when the Rappahannock River near Fredericksburg, Virginia, was "dotted with such a fairy fleet."

Both sides frequently swapped insults, which they termed "smart talk" or "jawing." During the long siege of Vicksburg, a Confederate shouted across the lines, "When is Grant going to march into Vicksburg?" and received the reply, "When you get your last mule and dog ate up."

Dealings between enemy soldiers were not confined to banter or barter. Foes meeting in the no man's land between the lines might act in a spirit of simple kindness. On one occasion, two unarmed Confederates of the 12th Georgia, carrying a wounded comrade to the hospital, stumbled upon a Federal picket. Instead of demanding their surrender, the Federal directed the men back toward their own lines. Sometimes, pickets of both sides met surreptitiously to drink and play cards. And after battles, burial details often found themselves rubbing shoulders with the enemy as they collected and buried their fallen comrades. One Southern detail lacked sufficient shovels and had to borrow some from Federals performing the same grim task. Once the men started talking on occasions such as these, they would often show each other family pictures and letters from their loved ones back home.

Soldiers found a common ground in music, and rival bands were known to serenade each other from opposing camps. At

Federal and Confederate pickets lift a Christmas toast to each other from opposite sides of a stream.

Fredericksburg, Federal musicians played a medley of Northern airs. "Now give us some of ours," Confederates hollered from across the river. Obligingly, the band swung into "Dixie," "My Maryland" and "Bonnie Blue Flag." The concert closed with both sides singing "Home Sweet Home" at the top of their lungs.

Such displays of comradeship were strictly against regulations, of course. But many officers winked at the infringements, taking the view that a little friendliness was harmless so long as the men did their duty when the battle call sounded.

Besides, the officers themselves were far from guiltless. A number of them had been on good terms in the prewar Army and were quick to show their respect for their old companions. General Ulysses S. Grant, on learning at Petersburg, Virginia, that the

bonfires along the Confederate line were in celebration of General George Pickett's newborn son, ordered his own troops to light similar congratulatory fires and sent his old Mexican War comrade a child's silver service through the lines. In occupied Williamsburg, Virginia, during the spring of 1862, Union cavalry officer George Armstrong Custer served as best man at the wedding of a West Point classmate, a prisoner of the Federals. Custer wore the blue dress uniform of a Federal Army captain; the bridegroom appeared in the gray dress uniform of a Confederate Army captain.

Many men in both Armies would have heartily agreed with the Confederate soldier who, after a long talk with a Federal between the lines, wrote home wistfully, "We could have settled the war in 30 minutes had it been left to us."

Once the battle was joined, the fighting became chaotic. Amid the thick smoke, the crash of musketry and cannonfire, the shouts and screams of the fighting and dying, a soldier knew little of what was happening except for what he saw directly ahead of him. "The air was filled with a medley of sounds, shouts, cheers, commands, oaths, the sharp reports of rifles, the hissing shot, groans and prayers," recalled a private from the 20th Maine. Sergeant Major Elbridge Copp of the 3rd New Hampshire recorded his view of the chaos: "Some of the men, with faces blackened by the powder from the tearing open of cartridges with the teeth in the act of loading their rifles, looked like demons rather than men, loading their guns and firing with a fearful, fiend-like intensity; some of the boys would load and fire with deliberation, while others, under an intense, insane excitement, would load and fire without aim."

Amid the din, soldiers might not be able to hear their guns go off; a man could go through all the motions of ramming a new load down his rifle barrel without noticing that the previous round had misfired. After three days of fighting at Gettysburg, victorious Federals found on the battlefield 12,000 rifles containing two unfired cartridges, and about 6,000 that held between three and 10 loads. It is just as well that the weapons misfired, for the resultant explosion would have been a good deal more harmful to those firing than to their enemy. Some men would forget to remove the ramrod before pressing the trigger, sending the rod sailing through the air.

In the heat of battle, a soldier might leap atop a parapet to shriek defiance at the enemy. Others would beg for the privilege of carrying the regimental colors — the most dangerous duty of all — or take command when all their officers were wounded, or even refuse to leave the field when struck down. It was only after the battle that many of the men gave in to tension, exhaustion, grief and revulsion. "When the fight was over and I saw what was done the tears came free," a soldier wrote home to his wife. "To think of civilized people killing one another like beasts one would think that the supreme ruler would put a stop to it."

From a soldier of the 6th Georgia came a poignant indictment. "None can realize the horrors of war, save those actually engaged," he wrote. "The dead lying all around, your foes unburied to the last, horses and wagons and troops passing heedlessly along. The stiffened bodies lie, grasping in death, the arms they bravely bore, with glazed eyes, and features blackened by rapid decay. Here sits one against a tree in motionless stare. Another has his head leaning against a stump, his hands over his head. They have paid the last penalty. They have fought their last battle. The air is putrid with decaying bodies of men and horses. My God, My God, what a scourge is war."

Victors and vanquished alike were subject to the aftershock of battle. Once the fighting ended, many soldiers found themselves unable to stand, much less march. The unutterable weariness could linger long after the engagement, a fact that may help explain why generals who had won a battle sometimes declined to immediately pursue the enemy.

As the soldiers marched on from one bloodstained field to another, they no longer reacted as farm boys, clerks or students but as veterans, hardened to war's horrors, and resolved to carry on. "I see no reason to dread

In this previously unpublished photograph, soldiers in General William Brooks's division of the Federal VI Corps bivouac in reserve on the west bank of the Rappahannock River during the Second Battle of Fredericksburg in 1863. Shortly after the photograph was taken, some of these men were killed in the fighting around Salem Church.

the future," the 14th Iowa's Peter Wilson wrote to his father in January 1863. "I trust that the Almighty hand that has kept me in health thus far will keep me still in safety although much danger may be before me. If it is God's will that I find my grave in the South I hope to be ready. Let it come when it may, I am determined to do my duty and come home honorably or never."

Many on both sides were that determined. As soldiers, they were never polished, but they were among the best fighters that America has ever produced. They stayed at their task until it was done, however distasteful army life was to them.

Ironically, it was Braxton Bragg, a general despised by the rank and file of the Confederate Army for his callous use of troops, who best eulogized the qualities of the Civil War fighting man. "We have had in a great measure to trust to the individuality and self-reliance of the private soldier," he wrote after the fearful Battle of Stones River during the winter of 1862-1863. "Without the incentive or the motive which controls the officer, who hopes to live in history; without the hope of reward, and actuated only by a sense of duty and of patriotism, he has, in this great contest, justly judged that the cause was his own, and gone into it with a determination to conquer or die." However much credit and glory might be given to the leaders in this War, Bragg felt assured that "history will yet award the main honor where it is due — to the private soldier."

Winslow Homer's View of the War

At the outset of the War, the prestigious illustrated journal *Harper's Weekly* commissioned a young freelance artist named Winslow Homer *(right)* to record the life of soldiers at the front. Homer first observed the men of General George B. McClellan's Army of the Potomac as they underwent training around Washington in 1861; he then rejoined the Federal troops in 1862 as they laid siege to Yorktown on the Virginia Peninsula. During these periods, he traveled with his cousin, Colonel Francis Channing Barlow, commander of the 61st New York, and often used the soldiers of that regiment as subjects for his sketches. In addition to his work for *Harper's*, he produced a raft of studies that he later developed into oil paintings in his studio in New York City. Altogether, his wartime labors yielded 180 sketches, wood engravings, watercolors and oils.

Homer's depictions, 15 of which appear on these pages, reached a wide and appreciative audience. One of his war paintings, a stark and forceful view of Barlow confronting three Confederate captives *(pages 168-169)*, created a sensation when it was exhibited in 1866 alongside the more sentimental studies that were fashionable at the time. For such work, Homer won high praise from critics; one of them lauded him as being among the few artists "who had endeavored to tell us any truth about the war." Of his personal feelings and experiences during his *Harper's* assignment, Homer said nothing (throughout his life he was grudging about biographical information); but with pencil, pen and paintbrush, few men were ever more eloquent.

In a wood engraving *(right)* published by *Harper's Weekly* in 1862, Winslow Homer portrayed joyful soldiers receiving Christmas gifts from home. *Harper's* made and printed more than 35 wood engravings from Homer's sketches during the War years.

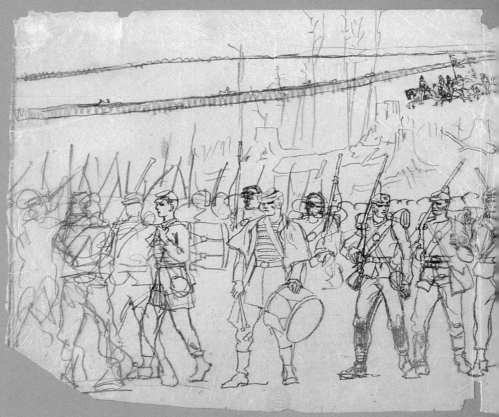

AN INFANTRY COLUMN ON THE MARCH

RESTING MULES TETHERED TO A WAGON

AN ARMY WAGON

STUDIES OF INFANTRYMEN

CAVALRYMAN

AN ARMY ENCAMPMENT

A SOLDIER LOADING A RIFLE

DRUMMER

A BUGLER AND DRUMMERS SOUND REVEILLE

A YOUNG SOLDIER

ZOUAVES PITCHING HORSESHOES

TWO CAVALRYMEN CHASING A GOOSE

PRISONERS FROM THE FRONT